Zora!

The Life of
Zora Neale Hurston

Judith Bloom Fradin

« and »

Dennis Brindell Fradin

Clarion Books
Houghton Mifflin Harcourt
Boston • New York • 2012

Clarion Books

215 Park Avenue South

New York, New York 10003

Clarion Books is an imprint of
Houghton Mifflin Harcourt Publishing Company.

www.hmhbooks.com

The text was set in Truesdell Std.
Book design by Greta D. Sibley

Library of Congress Cataloging-in-Publication Data
Fradin, Judith Bloom.
Zora! : the life of Zora Neal Hurston / Judith Bloom Fradin and Dennis Brindell Fradin.
p. cm.
Includes bibliographical references.
ISBN 978-0-547-00695-6
1. Hurston, Zora Neale—Juvenile literature. 2. Authors, American—20th century—Biography—Juvenile literature.
3. African American authors—Biography—Juvenile literature. 4. African American women—Biography—Juvenile
literature. 5. Folklorists—United States—Biography—Juvenile literature. I. Fradin, Dennis B. II. Title.
PS3515.U789Z69 2012
813'.52—dc23   [B]
2011025949

Manufactured in China
LEO 10 9 8 7 6 5 4 3 2 1
4500355386

For our lovely grandchildren—Aaron, Anna, Benjamin, Olivia,
and Ariana Fradin and Shalom and Dahlia Richard

«« ◆ »»

CONTENTS

«« ◆ »»

»»» Upon her return to New York, Zora demonstrated the
Crow Dance she learned in the Bahamas.

INTRODUCTION

«« ◆ »»

"I'll Say My Say and Sing My Song"

FROM BEGINNING TO END, Zora Neale Hurston's life was extraordinary. She packed so much into her sixty-nine years that we might even say her "lives" were extraordinary.

Zora spent her childhood in the all-black town of Eatonville, Florida. Because she didn't experience prejudice until she left Eatonville as a teenager, Zora grew up proud to be black and unaware of racism. As a little girl, she was so confident of her specialness that she believed the moon followed her wherever she went. Zora's confidence remained with her all her life and sustained her through many tough times.

Zora decided to make writing her career. She traveled through the American South, as well as the islands of the West Indies, collecting folklore, which she transformed into nonfiction books. She also wrote novels. Despite numerous rejections, Zora eventually had seven of her books published during her lifetime, as well as many stories and articles.

Zora was passionate about her writing. She broke off her relationship with a man to whom she referred as "the real love affair of my life" because he wanted her to give up writing and marry him. She didn't mind the marrying part — she was married and divorced three times — but forsaking her writing career was out of the question. Zora was also known to fight with reviewers who criticized her work, and she ended her close friendship with the author Langston Hughes over a literary dispute.

None of Zora's books sold more than a few thousand copies while she was alive, and as a result she didn't earn much of a living from her writing. The largest royalty check she ever received from the sale of her books was only $943.75, and she earned such a meager income from her books that she had to take on other jobs. At various times she worked as a maid, doctor's receptionist, personal assistant to a singer, waitress, caretaker to an invalid, manicurist, secretary, college drama teacher, collector of folk music, editor for a government publication, Hollywood script consultant, lecturer, college literature teacher, paid political worker, explorer, ghostwriter, newspaper reporter, librarian, and high school English teacher.

Often Zora could barely support herself, and sometimes she descended into abject poverty. One day in March 1951, she counted "four pennies" as all the money she had in the world. There were times when she had to pawn her typewriter just to buy groceries. To make matters more difficult, she suffered from a long list of illnesses, including heart and intestinal ailments.

Through it all, Zora continued to write, never losing faith that great success waited just around the corner. Almost until the day she suffered a fatal stroke in a Florida charity home, she worked on a book that had occupied her for most of the 1950s, fervently believing that it would revive her career. It didn't, but more than a decade after her death Zora was rediscovered by a new generation of readers who admired her writing and her unconquerable spirit.

"Servants Are Servants"

ON JANUARY 15, 1950, Zora Neale Hurston celebrated her fifty-ninth birthday. By then she was one of the nation's most accomplished authors. She had four novels to her credit, including her best-known work, *Their Eyes Were Watching God*. Hurston had also published two books of folklore, an autobiography, and numerous short stories and articles. She had won awards, spoken at universities, and been friends with Langston Hughes, Fannie Hurst, and other leading authors of her era.

Zora's books didn't sell very well during her lifetime, however. The result was that she was broke — or nearly so — most of her adult life. She was so impoverished in early 1950 that she took a job as a maid in the ritzy Miami suburb of Rivo Alto Island. For thirty dollars a week, plus food and a room in which to sleep, Hurston cooked and cleaned for the Burritts. The white couple liked the middle-aged black servant, but they didn't suspect that their "girl Zora" was a noted author until Mrs. Burritt was leafing through the March

18, 1950, *Saturday Evening Post.* Beginning on page 22 of that popular magazine was a story titled "Conscience of the Court" by Zora Neale Hurston.

Zora was dusting off the bookshelves in the next room when she was summoned to talk to Mrs. Burritt. Yes, Zora admitted, she had written the *Saturday Evening Post* story. Mrs. Burritt asked Zora more questions and was astonished to learn that the woman who washed her family's floors and cooked their meals had taught college and had worked as a movie writer in Hollywood. The Burritts were so amazed by their maid's achievements that they called the *Miami Herald.* The newspaper sent out the reporter James Lyons, who interviewed Mrs. Burritt and Zora, then wrote an article titled "Famous Negro Author Working as Maid Here Just 'to Live a Little.'" The article, which appeared in the March 27 *Miami Herald,* began:

> *Employed as a maid in a Rivo Alto Island home is one of the nation's most accomplished Negro women. She is Zora Neale Hurston, 42, author of seven books published in six languages. You'll find her listed in Who's Who—one of the handful of her race so honored. As a domestic, she explained, she is getting a needed "change of pace." She isn't down on her luck....Why, now, is she working as a maid?*

She was temporarily "written out," Zora responded. "You can only use your mind so long. Then you have to use your hands. A change of pace is good for everyone. I like to cook and keep house. Why shouldn't I do it for somebody else awhile? A writer has to stop writing every now and then and just live a little."

Zora was embarrassed for her friends in the Miami area to read that she was employed as a maid. It only got worse. A month after the *Miami Herald* article appeared, the *St. Louis Post-Dispatch* published a longer version of the James Lyons article.

> One of the nation's most accomplished Negro women is now working in a swank Gold Coast home. Press the doorbell at her fashionable Rivo Alto Island address and she will appear to greet you — in uniform. Miss Zora Neale Hurston, distinguished author of seven books published in six languages, is presently employed as a maid.

Soon newspapers throughout the country picked up and expanded upon the articles. Just as she had shaved seventeen years off her true age when interviewed by James Lyons, Zora concocted a variety of stories to explain why she was working as a maid. Her main story was what she told Lyons—that she was "written out" and needed "a change of pace."

To others who inquired, she said that her work as a maid was actually research. She needed to learn firsthand what working as a maid was like because she was planning to start a magazine "for and by" domestic workers. To Burroughs Mitchell, her editor at Charles Scribner's Sons publishing house, she wrote, "All I wanted was a little spending change when I took this job." She made up yet another explanation for her employers. She had large sums of money in banks in Europe, she told the Burritts, but since she didn't want to dip into her savings, she was working for them.

Her explanations didn't fool the *Amsterdam News*, a black-owned newspaper in New York City, where Zora had lived for many years. Zora was working as a maid for the same reason anyone else did, this newspaper concluded. "Although Miss Hurston is one of our best-known writers, she never did make a reasonable pile of money."

It evidently made the Burritts uncomfortable to know that the woman who kept house for them was a person of distinction. "Servants are servants and must act accordingly unless the whole traditional relationship of employer and employee is to be endangered," Mrs. Burritt was quoted as saying by James Lyons. Zora soon left her job as the Burritts' maid — probably by mutual agreement. Characteristically making the best of the situation, Hurston told her editor that all the publicity had actually been good for her.

"My working [as a maid] is causing a tremendous sensation in Miami," she wrote to Burroughs Mitchell. "I am being lectured about at poetry and other literary clubs. [A radio] announcer devoted half his time to me over the air last week. I have offers to do some 'ghosting.' It certainly has turned out to be one slam of a publicity do-dad."

Despite her efforts to put on a cheerful face, the truth was that Zora Neale Hurston was nearly sixty years old, in failing health, without a permanent home, and badly in need of the thirty dollars a week she no longer received. The good news was, she was once again pursuing her number one passion in life: writing.

2

"The Moon Ran After Me"

FOR MOST OF HER LIFE, Zora Neale Hurston lied about her age. She told reporter James Lyons that she was forty-two when she was actually fifty-nine years old. At various times Zora claimed to have been born in 1895, 1898, 1899, 1900, 1901, 1902, 1903, 1904, or 1908. The most outrageous birth-date she made up for herself was 1910 — shaving a whopping nineteen years off her true age. According to the Hurston family Bible, she was actually born on January 15, 1891, in Notasulga, a small Alabama town not far from the capital city of Montgomery. Zora was the fifth of eight surviving children — six boys and two girls — of John and Lucy Potts Hurston. The Hurstons were sharecroppers on a cotton plantation. Like many other poor southern people, they farmed a tract of land that belonged to another man and had to share their crop with him.

John and Lucy gave their new baby the long name Zora Neal Lee Hurston. The name Zora means "dawn" or "sunrise" in Slavic, a branch of European languages that includes Russian and Polish. How did her parents think of this odd name? In her autobiography, *Dust Tracks on a Road*, Hurston later speculated that her mother "had read it somewhere." The Neal in her name was in honor of a Mrs. Neal who was a friend of Zora's mother. Her second

»»» Zora's parents, John and Lucy Potts Hurston,
were sharecroppers in Alabama when Zora was born.

middle name, Lee, may have been for Lee County, along the border of which Notasulga is located. Zora later combined her two middle names to create Neale, and so she became known to history as Zora Neale Hurston.

When Zora was about a year old, her parents made a move that was to shape her entire life. As she explained in her autobiography: "The ordeal of share-cropping on a southern Alabama cotton plantation was crushing to [her father's] ambition." John Hurston heard that near Orlando in central Florida there was a remarkable new town. Called Eatonville, it had been founded in 1887 as an all-black community. John visited Eatonville and fell in love with the place. He settled his family there in 1892, when Zora was still a toddler.

At first the Hurston family lived in a small cabin in Eatonville, but they soon purchased a five-acre plot of land on which John, a skilled carpenter, built an eight-room house. Zora later remembered her Eatonville home as a paradise:

> There were plenty of orange, grapefruit, tangerine, guavas and
> other fruits in our yard. We had chicken on the table often; home-
> cured meat, and all the eggs we wanted. It was a common thing
> for us smaller children to fill the iron tea-kettle full of eggs and boil
> them, and lay around in the yard and eat them until we were full.
> Any leftover boiled eggs could always be used for missiles. There
> was plenty of fish in the lakes around the town, and so we had all
> that we wanted. We had oranges, tangerines and grapefruit to use
> as hand-grenades on the neighbors' children.

By the time the Hurstons settled there, the town of Eatonville was five years old and thriving. It had two churches, central Florida's only school for African American children, a post office, and a general store. It also had a library and a newspaper called the *Eatonville Speaker*.

John Hurston quickly made a success of himself in Eatonville. He established a carpentry business and on Sundays served as pastor of Macedonia Baptist Church. Zora's father wrote an early set of laws for Eatonville and also served as mayor of the town.

Because they lived in an all-black community, the young people of Eatonville didn't suffer from discrimination and name-calling that other black boys and girls had to endure. Zora grew up a self-confident and creative child. One of her early memories was her discovery that, wherever she went, the moon followed her. She became convinced that she was special in this regard: "The moon was so happy when I came out to play, that it ran shining and shouting after me like a pretty puppy dog. The other children didn't count."

Zora was shocked when her best friend, Carrie Roberts, claimed that the moon followed *her* wherever *she* went. No, Zora insisted, *she* was the moon's favorite child. To settle the dispute, one night Zora and her friend Carrie ran in opposite directions, keeping their eyes on the moon. That didn't solve a thing, for each girl still claimed that the moon had followed her as she ran.

Zora had a vivid imagination. "I was making little stories to myself, and have no memory of how I began," she later explained. "But I do remember some of the earliest ones."

One day Zora came in from playing outside and told her mother she had seen a bird sitting in the top of a pine tree with a tail so long that it stretched down to the ground. Zora claimed that she had climbed up the bird's tail into the tree, where she and the bird had a long talk. The strange creature told her that he had flown a long way just to speak to her. Another time, Zora confided to her mother that she had walked on top of a nearby lake without getting wet and that all the fish swimming beneath her feet had said hello to her.

Grandma Sarah Potts, who often came to Eatonville to visit, thought that Zora ought to be whipped for telling what she called lies. But Lucy was amused by Zora's tall tales and told her mother, "Oh, she's just playing."

Zora spent many hours with some miniature friends. She rescued the outer covering of an ear of corn from the garbage and turned it into a home-made doll she called Miss Corn-Shuck. Since her imaginary playmate seemed lonely, Zora swiped from her mother's dresser drawer a cake of scented soap, which became Mr. Sweet Smell. Some spools of thread from Lucy's sewing machine were transformed into the Spool People, and a loose doorknob that she yanked off became Reverend Door-Knob. Zora took all her play people into the open space beneath their house and had imaginary adventures with them over a period of years. Under Zora's direction the little folks held parties, carried on romances, had arguments, suffered illnesses, and went on trips together.

Zora was curious about the world beyond Eatonville. She climbed one of the chinaberry trees near her family's front gate and gazed out at the horizon. "It grew upon me that I ought to walk out to the horizon and see what the end of the world was like," she later wrote. She showed her friend Carrie the view from up in the chinaberry tree and together they planned to walk to the horizon. But when the morning they had chosen for their expedition arrived, Carrie didn't show up at their meeting place. She had gotten scared that the walk to the horizon would take all day and they might get lost.

Despite not being able to explore it just yet, Zora did manage to go a short way toward the horizon. In fact, because of her younger daughter's habit of wandering away from home, Lucy often said that on the day Zora was born someone must have sprinkled "travel dust" around their doorstep. A road leading to the city of Orlando ran past the Hurstons' house, and Zora liked to sit on the gatepost near the road and watch the white people drive by in their horse-drawn carriages and in a new invention called the automobile.

"Don't you want me to go a piece of the way with you?" Zora would call out to the occupants of the slow-moving vehicles. Often they would stop and let the pretty young black girl ride with them for a half mile or so. Then Zora would get out and walk back home.

Grandma Potts was angry when she heard about Zora asking white people for rides. She had once been a slave, and to her way of thinking, it was dangerous for a black person to act "forward" with white people. "Looking white folks right in the face!" Grandma Potts scolded. "They're going to lynch you yet. And don't stand in the doorway gazing out at them, neither. You're too brazen to live long."

Although her parents punished Zora whenever they discovered that she had ridden with strangers, her mother insisted that she didn't want to "squinch her spirit" lest she "turn out to be a mealy-mouthed rag doll by the time she gets grown." Lucy had another saying that she imparted to Zora and her other children. "Jump at the sun," she told them. "You might not land on the sun, but at least you will get off the ground."

Zora's parents knew that education was the key to jumping at the sun. Both of them could read and write well, which was unusual among African Americans at the time. Back in Alabama, Lucy had worked for a while as a country schoolteacher. Every night she gathered her young daughters and sons around her and taught them to read, write, and do arithmetic problems. The result was that by the time Zora entered Eatonville's Hungerford School she was far ahead of her classmates.

A highlight of her childhood occurred when Zora was in the fifth grade. Now and then white people from the North visited the Hungerford School to observe the students. One day two young white women from Minnesota came to hear Zora's class read aloud. The students were reading a story about Pluto, the ancient god of the underworld who kidnapped the beautiful goddess Persephone and carried her down to his dismal kingdom.

The story was difficult, and Mr. Calhoun, the teacher, squirmed as one child after another stumbled on the words. Finally it was Zora's turn. She had read and reread the myth of Pluto and Persephone in her reader, for it was one of her favorite stories. In fact, she had read the entire reader from cover to cover the first week of school. She read her paragraph aloud flawlessly, bringing a relieved smile to the face of Mr. Calhoun, who told her to continue reading the rest of the story.

After the class was dismissed, Zora was asked to remain in the room while the visitors conferred with Mr. Calhoun. The two young women from Minnesota were very impressed by Zora. They wanted her to visit them at the Park House hotel in nearby Maitland the next afternoon because they had a

»»» As a child, Zora attended Hungerford School in Eatonville, Florida.

surprise for her. Zora generally went around barefoot, even to school, but Mr. Calhoun informed her that she must wear shoes and stockings, and be spotless from head to toe, when she went to meet the ladies.

The next afternoon Zora was sent home from school an hour early. Her mother stood her in a tub filled with soapsuds and gave her a good scrubbing, then dressed her in her Sunday best — her red and white checked gingham dress, stockings, shoes, and a red ribbon in her hair. Her older brother, John Cornelius, then drove Zora by horse and buggy to the Park House in Maitland and waited outside while she visited with the two ladies.

The women, Miss Hurd and Mrs. Johnstone, gave Zora stuffed dates, preserved ginger, and other treats to eat. Then they asked her to read aloud from an issue of *Scribner's Magazine*. Zora read a passage from that adult magazine, drawing praise and smiles from the two women. After visiting with Zora for a few more minutes they sent her off with a gift — a heavy cylinder wrapped in fancy paper that they told her not to open until she reached home.

As soon as she and her brother entered their house, Zora opened her present. More than forty years later she still recalled the moment she saw what was inside:

> *Perhaps I shall never experience such joy again. The nearest thing*
> *to that moment was the telegram accepting my first book. One*
> *hundred goldy-new pennies rolled out of the cylinder. Their gleam*
> *lit up the world. It was not avarice that moved me. It was the*
> *beauty of the thing. I stood on the mountain. Mama let me play*
> *with my pennies for a while, then put them away for me to keep.*

The one hundred shiny pennies would be equal to about thirty dollars in today's money, but, as Zora wrote, it wasn't the value of the money that thrilled her. It was that the ladies thought she was special because of something she loved to do: read.

Those glittering pennies were just the beginning. The next day the ladies sent Zora a collection of fairy tales, a book of hymns, and a copy of *The Swiss Family Robinson*. A few weeks after returning to Minnesota, they sent Zora a large box filled with more books, including *Gulliver's Travels*, *Grimms Fairy Tales*, a story about Dick Whittington and his cat, a book of Greek and Roman myths, and a collection of Norse tales. Zora eagerly read the books and fell in love with the myths and folktales.

Reading wasn't the only way that Zora was exposed to stories. Her mother sent her on errands to Joe Clarke's general store, where the adults of Eatonville often sat out on the porch, holding what they called "lying sessions"— what today we would call storytelling. Holding the bag of sugar or spools of thread that she had been sent to buy, Zora would listen to the adults talk. She heard stories about God and the devil, about how black people got their color, and about High John the Conqueror, Brer Fox, and Sis Snail—some of which went back to slavery days. She also heard some old African American sayings, like "I got a rainbow wrapped and tied around my shoulder" to express happiness, and "I have been in sorrow's kitchen and licked out all the pots" to express sadness.

Many years later, Zora recalled that when she became moody as a child she would "go hide under the house away from the rest of the family and mood away." For the most part, though, Zora in her early years was "wrapped in rainbows." She played baseball, "holding down first base on the team" with her brothers and their friends, she later wrote. She felt an attachment to the woods, flowers, and people of her hometown. She had a close family, a warm home life, and books to read.

But when Zora was thirteen years old, her pleasant childhood would come to an abrupt end.

"In Sorrow's Kitchen"

BY LATE SUMMER OF 1904, Zora's mother was very ill. "I knew that Mama was sick," Zora wrote in her autobiography. "She kept getting thinner and thinner and her chest cold never got any better. Finally, she took to bed." Lucy Potts Hurston may have been suffering from tuberculosis, a lung disease.

On September 19, 1904, Lucy called Zora to her bedside. She had an important request to make of her younger daughter. When a bedridden person was about to die, the people of Eatonville followed some old southern superstitions. For one thing, they removed the pillow from under the patient's head, in the belief that its false comfort would only prolong the agony of dying. For another, the bed containing the patient was turned toward the east, so that the dying person would awaken in the afterlife facing the rising sun. Clocks in the room were covered, because — it was thought — any timepiece looked upon by the dying person wouldn't work anymore. Mirrors were also covered. Some claimed this was to prevent the dying person's ghost from attaching itself to the looking glass. It was also believed that anyone who saw his or her reflection in the mirror at the instant the sick person died would be death's next victim.

Barely able to talk, Lucy Potts Hurston rasped out her last request to Zora. She didn't believe in the old superstitions, she said. When the time came for her to die, she didn't want the pillow taken from beneath her head. She didn't want the clock or the looking glass in her room covered. Neither did she want her bed moved to face the east.

"I promised her as solemnly as nine years could do, that I would see to it," Zora wrote in her autobiography. Actually, Zora was thirteen years old at the time, but this was still an enormous responsibility for a girl so young.

Zora left Mama's bedside for a little while and was playing outside when she noticed a number of her mother's friends entering the house. She ran back into the room and saw people crowded around the bed as her mother struggled to breathe. Before Zora could do anything about it, her father and some others lifted the bed and turned it toward the east. Zora tried in vain to prevent them from following the old customs.

"Don't take the pillow from under Mama's head!" Zora cried. "She said she didn't want it moved! Don't cover up that clock! Leave that looking glass like it is!"

But John held Zora back so that the usual customs could be carried out. A little while later Lucy tried to say something—Zora thought her mother was trying to speak to her—and a few minutes after that, she took her last breath.

"Mama died at sundown and changed a world," Zora later recalled.

Her father had always seemed so strong to Zora, but without Lucy, he was a lost soul. For days he walked aimlessly around the house saying, "Poor thing! She suffered so much." Zora was suffering, too. Besides having to deal with her loss, she felt guilty for failing to keep her promise to her mother. "I was to agonize over that for years to come," she confessed in her autobiography. "In the midst of play, in wakeful moments after midnight, on the way home from parties, and even in the classroom during lectures."

At the time of their mother's death, Zora's siblings ranged in age from twenty-two-year-old Bob to six-year-old Everett. John decided that the best thing for Zora would be to enroll her in the Florida Baptist Academy, a boarding school in Jacksonville that Zora's fifteen-year-old sister, Sarah, attended. So, two weeks after her mother's funeral, Zora packed a few clothes into an old trunk and was driven to Maitland by her brother Dick. There she boarded the midnight train. "I was on my way from the village, never to return to it as a real part of the town," she later wrote. By morning she had completed the 135-mile journey.

Zora learned something in Jacksonville: The rest of the world was not like Eatonville. "Jacksonville made me know that I was a little colored girl," she later recalled. Like other black people, she was not welcome in certain stores. She was expected to go to the back of streetcars. She heard white people call African Americans insulting names, and she was probably called those names herself.

Except for arithmetic, Zora did well in her classes during her year at the Florida Baptist Academy. She earned good grades, and when the city of Jacksonville held a spelling bee for its "Negro schools," Zora came in first place. As Jacksonville's "Negro spelling champion," Zora was presented with a world atlas, a Bible, and so much cake and lemonade that she thought she could feel it coming out of her skin.

But other aspects of school life were disheartening for Zora. She was one of the youngest students at the academy, and the other girls who had lived for a time in the growing city poked fun at her country way of speaking and old-fashioned style of dress. Events 135 miles away in her hometown also contributed to Zora's unhappiness in Jacksonville.

On February 14, 1905 — one month after Zora's fourteenth birthday — John Hurston remarried. His new bride, Mattie Moge Hurston, was only twenty years old, making her just six years older than Zora and three years younger than Zora's oldest brother, Bob. The Hurston children were upset that John had remarried just five months after their mother's death to a woman less than half his age.

Zora's sister, Sarah, was the first to voice her resentment. Around the time of John's remarriage, Sarah became ill and returned home to recuperate. Enraged at finding that she had a new stepmother, Sarah made some remarks about the marriage coming too soon after Lucy's death. Mattie Moge Hurston convinced her husband to whip sixteen-year-old Sarah for her comments. Furthermore, Sarah was not allowed to continue at the Florida Baptist Academy and her father threw her out of the house. Soon after, Sarah married and settled in another Florida town, taking the youngest child in the family, seven-year-old Everett, with her.

When Lucy was alive, John Hurston had made it clear that Sarah was his favorite child. He had always given Sarah everything she wanted, whether it

»»» This may be the earliest known photo of Zora Neale Hurston, taken, perhaps, soon after she arrived in Jacksonville. It is not known when or where this picture was taken, but Zora looks quite young, doesn't she?

was toys, clothes, or music lessons. Whipping Sarah and evicting her from the family home was so out of character for John that his children all blamed his new wife for putting him up to it.

Zora also blamed Mattie at least partly for what happened to her. One day the assistant principal of the Florida Baptist Academy called Zora into her office and told her some troubling news. Her father had not sent the money to pay her room and board. If he didn't pay soon, Zora would have to leave the academy. Every few days after that, the assistant principal cornered Zora and spoke to her about the unpaid bill. Several times Zora was outside in the schoolyard with her friends when the assistant principal yelled out the window about her father's debt to the school.

Zora was afraid that she would be kicked out of the academy, but the school found another way for her to work off the debt. She was put to work cleaning up the school's kitchen and pantry every day after classes. On Saturdays, she had to scrub the school's staircases.

When the school year ended in the springtime, Zora received another terrible shock. Her father didn't come to pick her up, and neither did he send money for Zora to pay her own way home. This time the assistant principal felt sorry for Zora. She lent her a dollar and a half so that she could travel home by steamboat and train.

Zora's homecoming was not a happy one. "So I came back to my father's house which was no longer home," she recalled in her autobiography. "The very walls were gummy with gloom. Papa's children were in his way, because they were too much trouble to his wife."

It didn't take long for Zora to have an argument with her stepmother. Upon her marriage, Lucy had taken her prize possession, a feather bed, from her parents' home. She had promised Zora that her special bed would one day be hers. When Zora returned home to find that Mattie was sleeping in this bed, it was more than she could bear. To prevent their stepmother from sleeping in the feather bed any longer, Zora and her younger brother Clifford Joel removed and hid the mattress.

Mattie discovered that Zora was behind this prank and tried to convince John to whip her for what she had done. Zora's father didn't seem to know what to do. He probably felt deeply wounded that his whole family was turning against him, for Zora's siblings all took her side as she continued to defiantly lay claim to the feather bed. In fact, Zora's brother John Cornelius and their father nearly got into a fistfight over the matter.

After that, the other children moved out of the family home and had little to do with their father for the rest of his life. John Cornelius rented a room in a boardinghouse in Jacksonville and went to work in a fish processing plant. Bob moved into the same boardinghouse and obtained a job as a nurse at a "Negro hospital." Zora's brother Dick married and settled in Sanford, Florida. Zora, Clifford Joel, and Benjamin were sent to live with various friends of their mother's.

For the next seven years — starting with her leaving home in 1905 all the way until 1912 — we know few details about Zora's activities. No known letters from this segment of her life have been found. Without providing specific information, Zora's autobiography makes it clear that she was "in sorrow's kitchen" during these years. "I was shifted from house to house of

»»» In 1905, about five months after Lucy Hurston died, John Hurston
married twenty-year-old Mattie. Zora was fourteen at the time.

relatives and friends and found comfort nowhere," she wrote. "I was miserable. I was in school off and on."

We do know that during this period Zora sometimes worked as a maid for white families in various Florida towns. Heartbroken that her formal schooling seemed to be over at age fourteen, she did what she could to educate herself by reading her employers' books at every opportunity. As a result, she wasn't a very good maid. "No matter how I resolved, I'd get tangled up with their reading matter, and lose my job," she later revealed. "It was not that I was lazy, I just was not interested in dusting and dishwashing."

We also know about a memorable incident that occurred around 1911, when Zora was about twenty years old. At the time, she was back in Eatonville, temporarily living with her father and stepmother. John Hurston apparently hoped that his daughter and wife would make a truce. That was not possible, though, for Zora still hated Mattie and blamed her for splitting her family apart.

One Monday morning Zora said something that Mattie found insulting. Mattie tried to convince John to punish Zora for what she had said, but he refused to take sides between his wife and daughter. Mattie struck back. Calling Zora a "sassy, impudent heifer," Mattie picked up a bottle and threw it toward Zora's head. "She never should have missed," Zora later wrote.

Zora flew into a tremendous rage. She slammed Mattie against the wall and began pounding her stepmother's face with her fists. Mattie tried to defend herself by yanking her stepdaughter's hair and clawing at her neck and arms, but Zora had grown up fighting with her brothers and their friends, and the scratching and hair-pulling hardly fazed her. As Zora continued to punch her,

Mattie begged her husband for help, but he was so disturbed by the fight that he just stood by the doorway and wept. Finally, Mattie fell helplessly to the floor and John pulled Zora away before she could beat her any further.

Upon regaining consciousness, Mattie asked John Hurston to have Zora arrested. He refused to do that, too. Soon after, John and Mattie Moge Hurston were divorced. Not even thirty years later when she was an accomplished author and anthropologist did Zora show any regret for having beaten up her stepmother. She was only sorry, she wrote, that she hadn't "finished the job." And although she later confessed to feeling "sorry for him," Zora never forgave her father for his role in the breakup of the Hurston family.

4

"The Golden Stairs"

FOLLOWING THE FIGHT with her stepmother, Zora's life began to gradually improve. She moved out of her home in Eatonville — this time permanently. She found better jobs. For example, she was hired to work as a doctor's receptionist. She answered the telephone and ran his office so efficiently that the doctor offered to pay for her training as a practical nurse.

Zora was considering the offer when she received a letter from her oldest brother. Bob was studying at Meharry Medical College, a school for African Americans in Nashville, Tennessee. Married with three children, Bob wanted Zora to come live with him and his family while he finished at Meharry and established himself as a physician. In exchange for Zora helping his wife, Wilhelmina, run the household, Bob promised to send his sister to high school.

Attending high school was something few black southerners of the early 1900s were able to do. In fact, as late as 1916 there were only about sixty public high schools for African Americans in the entire southern United States.

»»» Zora lived with her brother, Robert, his wife, Wilhelmina, and their children between 1912 and 1913.

At that time, only three of every one hundred African American youths in the South attended high school. Twenty-one-year-old Zora was past the usual high school age, but the chance to resume her education was a big reason she packed her bags and caught the train to Nashville.

"Nothing can describe my joy," she wrote in her autobiography. "I was going to have a home again. I was going to school. I was going to be with my brother!"

However, more disappointment awaited her in Tennessee. Shortly after Zora's arrival at her brother's home, he told her that he couldn't send her to high school right away. She was needed around the house too much for her to

»»» An unhappy-looking Zora with her niece and nephews.

have time for that. But if Zora helped out for a little while, he would send her to high school as soon as possible.

Zora cooked, cleaned, and helped care for the three children as Wilhelmina recovered from what seems to have been a difficult childbirth. Shortly after graduating from Meharry in 1913, Bob moved his family, including Zora, to Memphis, Tennessee, where he set up a storefront office. Zora loved her brother and his family, and she knew that he truly intended to send her to school. But as time passed and nothing changed, Zora grew resentful. She was basically working as a maid again, she realized — only without being paid.

After living with Bob and his family for two or three years, Zora heard from a friend about a wonderful job opportunity. A young operetta singer needed a personal assistant, and the friend encouraged Zora to apply for the job.

Wearing a new blue dress, Zora went to meet the singer. "My feet mounted up the golden stairs as I entered the stage door of that theater," Zora later wrote. "The sounds, the smells, the back-stage jumble of things were all things to bear me up into a sweeter atmosphere. I felt like dancing towards the dressing room when it was pointed out to me."

At twenty-four, Zora was actually older than the blond, twenty-two-year-old "Miss M," as she referred to the singer in her autobiography. Perhaps this was when Zora first began to lie about her age, for she told Miss M that she was only fifteen years old. Zora looked so young that Miss M believed her.

The two young women liked each other immediately. Miss M told Zora what the job involved. She was to help Miss M in and out of her costumes, assist with her makeup, wash her stockings, run errands, and do other odds and ends for her.

"Well, Zora, I pay ten dollars a week and expenses," Miss M said. "You think that will do?"

When she heard *that*, Zora nearly fell over. Ten dollars in 1915 was equal to about two hundred in today's money and was probably a higher salary than Zora had received on any of her previous jobs. Zora informed her brother Bob of her good fortune and began a new life as Miss M's personal assistant.

At the time, movies and radio were in their infancy and television did not yet exist. Plays, lectures, and musical performances were among the leading forms of entertainment. Miss M belonged to a traveling troupe of performers who presented operettas—popular "light operas" that featured romantic stories with singing and dancing. When Zora began working for Miss M, the troupe was performing Gilbert and Sullivan's operetta *H.M.S. Pinafore*.

For the next year and a half, Zora worked for Miss M as the troupe moved from city to city performing in theaters in Tennessee, Pennsylvania, Massachusetts, Connecticut, Virginia, and Maryland. Those eighteen months were the most exciting time of Zora's life so far. She loved the theater—the singing and dancing and the audience's laughter and applause. And as they shared meals, lodged in the same hotels, and traveled together in the troupe's private train car, Zora became friendly with most of the thirty members of the company. Adopting her as a kind of kid sister, the troupe continually plied her with all the ice cream, soft drinks, and sweets she could consume. They also confided their secrets to Zora. They told her about their romances and about their dreams of becoming Broadway stars — if only someone would give them a chance.

In one town Miss M paid for Zora to take a crash course in manicuring. The troupe members then let her practice on them by trimming and polishing their nails. She became very good at manicuring nails — a skill that would prove useful for Zora a little later in life. Meanwhile, she was constantly reading. One of the male lead singers had attended Harvard University and had brought a suitcase full of books on the road with him. Noticing Zora's interest in his books, he lent some of them to her.

Like any kid sister, Zora was teased. Most of the troupe members were from the North and had never heard expressions like those Zora routinely used. They enjoyed listening to her "call names," and would tease her just to hear her refer to someone as a "mullet-headed, mule-eared, hog-nosed, gator-faced, goat-bellied, knock-kneed, razor-legged so and so."

The troupe doted on Zora because they believed her to be only fifteen or sixteen when actually she was in her midtwenties. Also, Zora was the only African American in the company. Because they were accustomed to working with people of various backgrounds, show business performers had long been known for their tolerance. As Zora later described it, the troupe members almost seemed to compete with one another over who could be friendliest to her.

Many years later, Zora declared, "I have no race prejudice of any kind." She attributed her attitude in part to her enjoyable experiences traveling with the operetta company. During that year and a half she became convinced that white people weren't so different from her friends and relatives in

Eatonville, or, as she once wrote, "I learned that skins were no measure of what was inside people."

Sometime in 1917, Miss M informed Zora that she was planning to get married and retire from the stage. She offered Zora some sound advice. Although Zora enjoyed traveling with the troupe, in the long run, Miss M insisted, it would be best for her to continue her education. Zora knew that Miss M was right. The troupe soon arrived for an engagement in Baltimore, where Zora's sister, Sarah, lived. There Zora ended her association with the operetta company. As a parting gift, Miss M gave Zora a cash bonus. Zora then said farewell to the troupe that had been like a family to her for the past eighteen months and began a new life in Baltimore.

The Hurston sisters were happy to be reunited and spent a lot of time together, but Zora did not move in with Sarah. Zora despised Sarah's husband, who she felt mistreated her sister. Zora once wrote that she wished him "a short sickness and a quick funeral."

To pay for groceries and a rented room, Zora went to work as a waitress in a Baltimore restaurant. She was making plans to enroll in night high school when she became quite ill. She was told that she needed to have her appendix removed. Since she couldn't pay for an operation, Zora entered the free ward of the Maryland General Hospital.

Emergency appendectomies were dangerous operations in those days. Just twenty-six years old, Zora realized that she might die without having achieved much in her life. She made a deal with the Almighty. If God would see her through the operation, she promised to "find the road that [she] must follow."

Zora was very slow to awaken from the anesthetic, but she survived the operation and was quickly up and about. She obtained another job waiting tables and enrolled in Baltimore's night high school for "colored youths." On her application she claimed to be sixteen years old, this time lopping a full decade off her true age.

Embarrassment at attending high school at the age of twenty-six wasn't the only reason she lied. According to Maryland state law, "all colored youths between six and twenty years of age" could enroll in public schools for free. If she admitted her true age, she would have had to pay for her schooling, which she could not afford.

Zora flourished at the night high school, excelling especially in English literature. She later wrote, "[Literature is] my world, and I shall be in it, if it is the last thing I do on God's green dirt-ball."

She did so well in high school that she decided to do something rare for a young black woman in the early 1900s. She made up her mind to attend college. In the fall of 1917 she entered Morgan Academy, the preparatory school for Morgan College in Baltimore.

Zora remained a student for the next decade and loved nearly every moment of it. She spent two years at Morgan Academy. There were eighteen students in her class — twelve young women and six young men — and besides being the oldest, Zora was the poorest. Her classmates, who came from the wealthiest and most influential African American families on the East Coast, had gorgeous clothes and plenty of spending money. Zora's wardrobe consisted of, in her own words, "one dress, a change of underwear and one pair of tan oxfords."

Anyone else in her position might have felt out of place at swanky Morgan

PUBLISHED BY THE PHILADELPHIA SOCIETY FOR NEGRO RECORDS & RESEARCH 1937

ZORA NEALE HURSTON

Anthropologist

Writer

Eatonville, Fla.

1903=

»»» This Zora photo was found in the Howard University Library Archives. Although she looks quite young in this picture, Zora was in her late twenties when she enrolled at Howard.

Academy. Not Zora. She hadn't forgotten her deal with God, and now that she had "found the road" that she must follow, she wasn't about to let a lack of underwear stop her! The other girls liked Zora and lent her clothes. In return, Zora, whom the girls called "Old Knowledge Bug," helped them with their schoolwork. Zora was so good a student that when the English teacher was absent, she was put in charge of running the class.

Once again, as at the Florida Baptist Academy, Zora ran short of funds. While Zora was still attending Morgan Academy, Dean William Pickens of Morgan College arranged for her to work as a caretaker for a white woman who had broken her hip. Grateful for the job, in 1917 or 1918, Zora wrote Dean Pickens a note of thanks. It is the earliest surviving letter we have of Zora's, and contains her first mention of her hopes to become a writer:

> *Dear Dean,*
> *Forty years hence, The world will look for someone that has really known you to write your biography. To see you as a husband and father, & have you as a friend and teacher, should mean that one would go beyond the superficial. I want to do that.*
> > *Yours Respectfully,*
> > *Zora Neale Hurston*

Zora planned to graduate from Morgan Academy and then enroll in Morgan College. But sometime in 1918 a young woman named May Miller visited her cousins Bernice and Gwendolyn Hughes at the academy. May was the daughter of Dr. Kelly Miller, an African American author, newspaper columnist, and dean of the College of Arts and Sciences at Howard University in Washington, D.C. At that time Howard was considered to be the premier center for higher education for African Americans. After spending a day with Zora, May Miller said to her, "Zora, you are Howard material. Why can't you come to Howard?"

Because she couldn't afford it, Zora answered.

"You can come and live at our house," said Zora's classmate Bernice Hughes, whose parents lived in Washington, D.C. "Then you won't have any room and board to pay. We'll rustle you up a job to make your tuition."

In June 1918, Zora withdrew from Morgan Academy and moved forty miles from Baltimore to Washington, D.C., presumably to live with the Hughes family as Bernice had offered. Two months after arriving in the nation's capital,

»»» In the fall of 1919, at the age of twenty-eight, Zora enrolled at Howard University in Washington, D.C.

Zora received some bad news. Her father, John Hurston, had been in Memphis, Tennessee, when the car he was driving was struck by a train, killing him. Zora refused to attend her father's funeral. Even in death, his youngest daughter didn't forgive him for marrying Mattie Moge and breaking up the Hurston family.

Howard University officials didn't think Zora was quite ready for college, so for her first year in Washington she attended Howard Academy, finally earning her high school diploma in May 1919 at the age of twenty-eight. That fall she entered Howard University, becoming a member of an elite group. At the time, the total black population in the United States was over ten million, of whom only about two thousand were enrolled in college.

Meanwhile, to help pay for her tuition, Zora had found work in the nation's capital. First she worked as a waitress at the Cosmos Club, an exclusive "white men only" club in downtown Washington. Over the years, the men who gathered at the Cosmos Club to socialize, order drinks, and play billiards included Theodore Roosevelt, who had been president of the United States from 1901 to 1909, Rudyard Kipling, an English author whose stories Zora had long admired, Alexander Graham Bell, the inventor of the telephone, and Woodrow Wilson, president of the United States from 1913 to 1921. Judging by how little she said about the experience in her autobiography, Zora didn't seem to have been much impressed by the rich and famous men she served there.

After her brief stint at the Cosmos Club, Zora put her training as a manicurist to good use. She was hired to trim nails in a men's barbershop on G Street. Knowing that she was a college student, her boss allowed her to work

»»» Zora waitressed at the Washington, D.C., Cosmos Club to help pay her tuition at Howard University.

from three thirty in the afternoon to eight thirty in the evening, which left her time for her university classes in the morning and for homework at night.

An event that she witnessed in the barbershop haunted Zora for the rest of her life. Zora's employer, George Robinson, was a black man who owned a string of barbershops in Washington. As was the custom in those days, Mr. Robinson's barbershops were segregated. Although all fifteen of its employees were black, only white men were allowed in as customers at the G Street shop. Mr. Robinson operated another barbershop, on U Street, for black customers.

One afternoon an African American man entered the G Street barbershop and sat down in an empty chair. "Haircut and shave!" he called out. None of the barbers paid attention to him. He then began talking about the Constitution and his rights as an American citizen. The barbers advised him to go to the U Street shop, but since he wouldn't budge, they picked him up and carried him out the door.

That night as she lay in bed, Zora thought about the afternoon's events. She knew that the black man had been right. The other employees had known it, too, she was certain. Why hadn't a single one of them taken the young man's side? Why, at the moment of truth, had Zora secretly been relieved that he was being thrown out of the shop?

The answer, she concluded, was that tending to the young black man would have provoked complaints from the other customers, perhaps costing the shop's employees their jobs. This was what had flashed through her own mind. But more than twenty years later when she wrote about the incident, Zora still felt guilty about having been afraid to do the right thing.

Although Zora had always been an excellent student, she did rather poorly academically at Howard. Her grades in English were good, but she received Cs and Ds in some other classes, and she even flunked Spanish and physical education. She was finding it increasingly difficult to keep up her studies while working. To make matters worse, she often lacked the money to pay her tuition. As a result, in the five years between 1919 and 1924 Zora completed only a year and a half of course work.

Yet in several ways her years at Howard were very fruitful. In 1920 she met a twenty-three-year-old fellow student named Herbert Sheen. Six years younger than Zora, Herbert was working his way through Howard as a waiter in the hope of one day becoming a doctor. He and Zora fell in love. "For the first time since my mother's death, there was someone who felt really close and warm to me," Zora later wrote. The couple would marry—but not for another seven years.

»»» Zora married medical student Herbert Sheen on May 19, 1927, then almost immediately set out on her folklore-documenting expedition. They divorced four years later, but remained friends throughout Zora's life.

Howard University was also where Zora began to write. "Home," a poem she wrote in 1919 about Eatonville, is one of her earliest known creations:

> *I know a place that is full of light,*
> *That is full of dreams and visions bright;*
> *Where pleasing fancy loves to roam*
> *And picture me once more at home.*
> *There nothing comes to mar my days,*
> *And dim for me the sun's loved rays;*
> *To shake my faith in things divine,*
> *and bare the cruelty of mankind.*
> *Oh! that I to that spot might flee!*
> *That peace and love might dwell with me*
> *And brush away the somber shrouds,*
> *And show the lining of the clouds!*

Zora submitted writing samples to the Howard University philosophy professor Dr. Alain Locke, who headed the school's literary club. Educated at Harvard University, and then at colleges in England, Germany, and France, Locke was one of the best-educated people in the United States. Even though, as a black man, he had experienced prejudice, Professor Locke reputedly had a bias of his own. He had such a low opinion of female students — so it was said — that on the first day of school he would offer the young women in his classes automatic Cs if they would *not come* to his lectures. But Zora was

»»» This photo, from the Moorland-Spingarn archives at
Howard University, could be a class photo of Zora,
who was thirty-three years old when she left the school.

accepted into the literary group and joined her acquaintance May Miller on the staff of the school's literary magazine, the *Stylus*.

In May 1921 Zora experienced one of the greatest thrills an author can have. That month her work appeared in print for the first time when the *Stylus* published her poem "O Night" and her story "John Redding Goes to Sea." Later would come fame and prizes, but the publication of her first poem and story in Howard University's literary magazine, when she was thirty, would always remain special to Zora because it marked the birth of her writing career.

"John Redding Goes to Sea" revealed Zora to be a writer of promise. The story's hero, a Florida youth, yearns to visit far-off lands and people. "No matter what he dreamed," Zora wrote, "he always ended by riding away to the horizon"—the same horizon that lured Zora as a child. John Redding's father, who once had similar dreams, sympathizes with him. But his mother refuses to let him go. Later, John is helping to repair a bridge when a storm strikes, causing a flood that sweeps him away. Zora concludes her story: "John Redding floated away toward the sea, the wide world—at last."

Zora's story set the pattern in several ways for her future work. Her characters in "John Redding" speak like the people Zora had known growing up in Eatonville. For example, John's mother complains, "He kain't help from wantin' to go rovin' cause travel dust been put down fuh him." Reading a sentence like that isn't easy, but having her characters talk like real people breathes life into them. Zora later became known for her realistic dialogue. Her love of travel and her vivid descriptions of nature also became hallmarks of Zora's writing style.

As a *Stylus* editor and a published author, Zora was invited to gatherings of the Saturday Nighters, a group of black writers that met in the Washington home of the poet Georgia Douglas Johnson. The group included W. E. B. Du Bois, whose book of essays, *The Souls of Black Folk*, is considered a classic of African American literature. Another Saturday Nighter was James Weldon Johnson, who had written the words to the song "Lift Every Voice and Sing," often called the African American national anthem. Professor Alain Locke was another participant. Zora's encounters with famous people at the Cosmos Club served her well, for she wasn't dazzled by these writers or afraid to speak up in their presence.

»»» Scholar, author, sociologist, professor, and civil rights advocate
W. E. B. Du Bois was one of the Saturday Nighters.

The evenings she spent with the Saturday Nighters convinced Zora that she could become a famous author, too. It happened that in New York City in 1923, Charles S. Johnson became editor of *Opportunity*, a new magazine that promised to portray "Negro life as it is." Johnson wrote to a number of professors at black colleges asking if they knew of talented young writers whose work would enhance his magazine. Professor Alain Locke replied by sending Johnson the issue of the *Stylus* that contained "John Redding Goes to Sea." Johnson liked Zora's story and wrote to her asking whether she had any others he might consider.

Zora had plenty of stories. She had run out of money and was spending most of her time working on the *Stylus*

»»» Songwriter, novelist, poet, professor, and NAACP president James Weldon Johnson attended the Saturday night gatherings, too.

and writing. She sent Johnson "Drenched in Light," a story about the exploits of a young Florida girl named Isis who liked to "sit atop of the gate post and hail the passing vehicles." Johnson published "Drenched in Light" in the December 1924 issue of *Opportunity*. This marked the first time Zora's work was presented to a national audience.

Opportunity's readers heaped so much praise on Zora's story that Mr. Johnson wrote to her with a suggestion. New York City was the center of America's publishing world. Zora should come to the big city and try to carve out a career for herself as a writer.

Zora knew that nine out of ten would-be authors who moved to New York wound up working as secretaries, elevator operators, or dishwashers. But she was now well into her thirties and financially unable to continue at Howard University. What did she have to lose? Besides, she had the inner confidence that she would be the one in ten who would succeed. Also, Zora's boyfriend, Herbert Sheen, had gone to Illinois to attend medical school. That was one less reason for her to stay in Washington, D.C.

Shortly before her thirty-fourth birthday, Zora packed her clothes, books, and stories, and took the train to the nation's biggest city. "So," she later recalled, "the first week of January, 1925, found me in New York with $1.50, no job, no friends, and a lot of hope."

"A Toe-Hold on the World"

DESPITE HAVING ONLY a dollar and a half in her pocket, Zora arrived in New York City at an opportune time. In 1925, the Big Apple, as the city was becoming known, was home to 6.3 million people, about 250,000 of whom were black. Of those quarter of a million African Americans, more than half lived in the neighborhood known as Harlem.

Harlem was like a city unto itself. It was nicknamed the "Capital of Black America" because African Americans around the country looked to Harlem for trends in civil rights, culture, business, entertainment, and fashion. From roughly 1920 to 1935 Harlem was the center of a remarkable burst of African American creativity in the arts. Although this movement spilled over into other U.S. cities, it was so closely linked to Harlem that it became known as the Harlem Renaissance.

At the heart of the Harlem Renaissance was an amazing outpouring of powerful literature. The writers included Langston Hughes, Countee Cullen,

»»» Children shared in the glory of the Harlem Renaissance. Here they carve soap in a sculpture class at the Harlem Art Workshop.

James Weldon Johnson, Wallace Thurman, W. E. B. Du Bois, and Alain Locke. Jazz also flourished in this period. Harlem Renaissance musicians included Louis Armstrong, Duke Ellington, Count Basie, Billie Holiday, Ethel Waters, Marian Anderson, and Jelly Roll Morton. Paul Robeson and Charles Gilpin were leading actors of the era. Zora would get to know most of the major figures of the Harlem Renaissance and would herself become one of its brightest stars.

But the Harlem Renaissance was more than a period when African Americans took great pride in their heritage. As the writer Arna Bontemps phrased it, during the Harlem Renaissance it was "fun to be a Negro." Or, to use a slang term of the 1920s, it was "hip" to be black.

Harlem was one of the country's most crowded neighborhoods. Yet its residents had a true touch of the pioneer spirit. Newcomers like Zora were

»»» Singer Ethel Waters and Zora became best friends in New York.

often helped by friends of friends and distant relatives. And with just $1.50 to her name, Zora certainly needed help. One of the first things she did upon her arrival was visit the office of Charles S. Johnson, the *Opportunity* editor who had suggested that she move to New York City. He arranged for Zora to lodge with friends at a Harlem apartment building. Later she found lodgings at a rooming house where young writers and artists were allowed to live rent-free.

Zora spent her first few months in Harlem writing stories and plays. She attended poetry readings and discussions of books at the 135th Street public library, and plays and lectures at the local YMCA. She renewed acquaintances with old friends such as Alain Locke and James Weldon Johnson, who were frequently in Harlem, and made many new friends among the other writers she met.

Zora also attended "rent parties." The host would invite friends and acquaintances to his or her apartment on a certain evening. On that night, dozens of people paid about fifty cents apiece to attend the party. The host would take in twenty dollars or more toward his or her rent. There would be plenty of food and drinks as well as live music. Zora loved to dance at the rent parties. Arna Bontemps recalled that Zora enlivened many a rent party by telling stories she had heard growing up in Eatonville. Sterling Brown, professor, poet, and literary critic, added that she had such a friendly and interesting personality that "when Zora was there, she *was* the party."

In the spring of 1925, Zora attended an event that would launch her career. Months earlier, Charles S. Johnson had announced that *Opportunity* magazine was holding a writing contest. It offered prizes for the best poems, plays, essays, and short stories by African American writers. Seven hundred entries were submitted, including several by Zora.

»»» Professor Alain Locke was another Saturday Nighter.

The award winners were announced at a large banquet held on Friday, May 1, 1925. The contest judges included Alain Locke, James Weldon Johnson, the popular novelist Fannie Hurst, and the famed playwright Eugene O'Neill. Also present were Annie Nathan Meyer, who had founded Barnard College for women in New York City in 1889 when she was only twenty-two years old, and the writer and photographer Carl Van Vechten.

Zora won four prizes. Fannie Hurst handed her the second place award for her story "Spunk." Zora also won honorable mention for her story "Black Death," second place for her play *Color Struck*, and honorable mention for another play, *Spears*. Her cash awards totaled seventy dollars — equal to about a thousand dollars in today's money. She was in good company, for the brilliant young writer Langston Hughes won the poetry award for "The Weary Blues."

Later that evening, Zora attended a party. She wore a long, bright-colored scarf over one shoulder. Zora wanted everyone to remember the name of her prize-winning play, so as she entered the room she flung the scarf around her neck and called out in a loud voice, "*Color Struck!*" Several people who witnessed this grand entrance resented Zora for showing off, but most got a kick out of her shameless self-promotion. Langston Hughes was so enthralled by her that he soon wrote to Carl Van Vechten: "Zora Neale Hurston is a clever girl, isn't she? I would like to know her." The truth was, although her many setbacks had toughened her, in many ways Zora was still the cheerful girl who believed that the moon followed her.

»»» Zora peeks out from behind a bush in the Barnard College Class of 1927 photo.

Shortly after the awards dinner, Annie Nathan Meyer asked Zora if she would like to attend Barnard, the college Meyer had founded. Zora jumped at the chance to continue college, especially since Mrs. Meyer said she would arrange a scholarship. Eleven days after the awards banquet,

Zora sent Annie Nathan Meyer a letter thanking her profusely for helping her get into Barnard and for showing interest in her:

> *My Dear Mrs. Meyer,*
> *I am tremendously encouraged now. My typewriter is clicking away till all hours of the night. I am striving desperately for a toe-hold on the world. You see, your interest keys me up wonderfully. I must not let you be disappointed in me.*
>
> *It is mighty cold comfort to do things if nobody cares whether you succeed or not. It is terribly delightful to me to have some one fearing with me and hoping for me, let alone working to make some of my dreams come true.*
>
> Zora Neale Hurston

A few months later, in September 1925, Zora entered Barnard as the college's only black student. At Barnard, she developed a keen interest in anthropology—the study of peoples and their cultures. In fact, she began taking anthropology classes at New York City's Columbia University, with which Barnard was affiliated. Her teachers, who included the famed anthropologist Franz Boas, gave Zora an unusual assignment.

At the time, some people claimed that black people's skulls were too small to hold normal-size brains. To disprove this theory, Zora stood on Harlem street corners with a measuring device called calipers. She would ask passing strangers, "Can I measure your head?" The poet Langston Hughes, who had become Zora's friend, explained, "Almost nobody else could stop the average

»»» Phrenology, the study of the size and shape of a person's head,
was popular in the 1920s. Some scientists tried to relate
such measurements to intelligence and morality.

Harlemite and measure his head with a strange-looking anthropological device
and not get bawled out, except Zora, who used to stop anyone whose head
looked interesting, and measure it." Zora was naturally friendly and at ease
with people, so passersby were willing to have their head placed in her measuring contraption.

Although Zora was selling some stories and articles to magazines, she received little money for her work, so she was very poor during this period. On October 17, 1925, she informed Annie Nathan Meyer, "Today I have 11 cents — all that is left of my savings. I must somehow pay my room-rent and I must have food." At about this time Zora was so impoverished that on one occasion she actually stole money from a blind beggar. According to the story, Zora had to go downtown. When she reached the subway station, she realized that she didn't have any money to pay her fare. A blind beggar approached her, but instead of putting money into his cup she took a few coins *out* for herself.

"I need money worse than you today," she reportedly told the beggar. "Lend me this. Next time I'll give it back."

Realizing that Zora was in dire need of financial assistance, Annie Nathan Meyer contacted Fannie Hurst, who had presented Zora with the award for her story "Spunk" at the *Opportunity* banquet. Like many others who had met Zora that night, Miss Hurst had found her to be a charming young woman. At the time, Fannie Hurst was one of the country's most popular writers — some claimed that she was *the* most popular author. Besides novels, she wrote magazine stories, screenplays, and newspaper articles, and she was often a guest on radio programs. Miss Hurst happened to be looking for an assistant, and in early November of 1925 she hired Zora to move into her home/office to be her live-in secretary.

Zora's duties included taking dictation in shorthand, typing manuscripts and letters, and filing important papers. Zora, who coined pet names for people she knew, nicknamed Miss Hurst "Genius" and liked her very much. But Zora didn't put her heart into the job. Twenty years later she told a friend, "My idea of Hell is that I would all through eternity be typing a book." Miss Hurst wasn't satisfied with Zora's work, saying that her "shorthand was short on legibility, her typing hit-or-miss, her filing a game of find-the-thimble." After about two months, Hurst fired Zora. Nonetheless, the two women remained friends. It appears that Zora continued to live in Hurst's home on and off for up to a year and that Miss Hurst contributed money to help support Zora's college education.

»»» Then-famous author Fannie Hurst mentored Zora in the mid-1920s.

Zora had done poorly as Fannie Hurst's secretary because she was more interested in writing her own stories than in typing and filing someone else's. In December 1925 Zora answered a Barnard College survey by declaring, "I have had some small success as a writer and wish above all to succeed at it." The next month Zora explained to Annie Nathan Meyer that she had missed a history exam at Barnard because she was daydreaming about her future as a writer instead of paying attention to the time of the test. "I shall try to lay my dreaming aside," she promised. "But, Oh, if you knew my dreams! my vaulting ambition!"

Zora gave up neither her dreams nor her vaulting ambition. Knowing that her former secretary yearned to become a successful author, Fannie Hurst read several of her stories and articles and offered suggestions for improving them. Zora made the changes halfheartedly, complaining to Mrs. Meyer that although she appreciated Miss Hurst's help, she preferred to find her own way as a writer. "I do not wish to become Hurstized," she explained. "There would be no point in my being an imitation Fannie Hurst." Miss Hurst even showed some of Zora's work to a few of her own editors at popular magazines. None of them accepted any of it for publication, but at least the editors became familiar with the stories and name of Zora Neale Hurston.

Meanwhile, *Opportunity* and other black-oriented magazines were publishing Zora's stories and articles. One of her most successful works of this period was "Muttsy." This short story about a Harlem gambler who falls in love with a young woman from Eatonville, Florida, won second place in the *Opportunity* writing contest in April 1926.

Within about a year of her arrival in New York, Zora became friends with Langston Hughes. Born in Joplin, Missouri, in 1902, Langston had moved around a lot. Following his parents' separation in his early childhood, he lived with his grandmother in Lawrence, Kansas, until the age of thirteen. His grandmother instilled in him the pride in being black, which became a feature of his writing. Langston later lived with his mother in Lincoln, Illinois, and in Cleveland, Ohio.

By the time he was in high school in Cleveland, Langston had begun writing poems, stories, and plays. One of his most famous poems, "The Negro Speaks of Rivers," was published in the *Crisis*, a magazine edited by W. E. B. Du Bois, when Hughes was only nineteen years old. Another famous Langston Hughes poem, "My People," was published in the *Crisis* two years later, in 1923:

> *My People*
> *The night is beautiful,*
> *So the faces of my people.*
> *The stars are beautiful,*
> *So the eyes of my people.*
> *Beautiful, also, is the sun.*
> *Beautiful, also, are the souls of my people.*

Like Zora, Langston Hughes came to Harlem in the mid-1920s. Just as he had hoped, Langston got to know the "clever girl" Zora Neale Hurston. In fact, Zora and the man she called "Lang" and sometimes "Bambino" became each other's best friend. The two had a lot in common. At a time when some

»»» The famous poet Langston Hughes was a young man
when he and Zora met in New York. The two
became best friends—for a while.

black authors fashioned characters who spoke, behaved, and tried to look like white people, Zora and Langston both took great pride in writing about black culture as they knew it. Both believed that "black is beautiful" forty years before the phrase became popular. Like Langston, Zora had spent much of her early life wandering from place to place. She would even name a chapter of her autobiography "Wandering," while he would call one of his two autobiographies *I Wonder as I Wander*.

There was one big difference in their personalities, however. Zora generally felt "drenched in light" and approached life cheerfully. Langston lacked confidence and was insecure about himself.

Because Zora and Langston grew so fond of each other, many people have assumed that there must have been a romance between them. That appears not to have been the case. The two up-and-coming writers seem to have limited their relationship to being close friends—what we might call "soul mates."

Like all writers, Zora, Langston, and their friends received a lot of rejection slips for their work. In the summer of 1926 they did what many aspiring writers have attempted. They began their own magazine. Called *Fire!!*, it claimed to be "devoted to the younger Negro artists"—meaning that it would publish its founders' work as well as that of other new black writers. The founders of *Fire!!* were Zora, Langston, Wallace Thurman, Gwendolyn Bennett, Bruce Nugent, and the artist Aaron Douglas. Each of the founders of *Fire!!* agreed to contribute fifty dollars (equal to $750 today) toward establishing the magazine. Only three of them actually scraped up the money they had promised. Zora was not one of them.

Some of the material for the magazine was stored in Zora's apartment. At the time, Zora's youngest brother, Everett, was staying with her. Just two days before *Fire!!* was to go to the printer, Everett Hurston searched his sister's apartment for some paper with which to start the fireplace. He found a pile of what he thought were old, discarded papers and used them to kindle the fire.

It turned out that the papers were the only copy of a short story Bruce Nugent had written for *Fire!!* When he learned that his story had gone up in flames, Nugent was very upset and angry at Everett. Since he didn't even have paper with which to rewrite the story, Nugent, in his own words, "took a roll of toilet paper and several paper bags and got on the subway and wrote the thing over again." Years later when the episode no longer stung so badly, Nugent said that he admired how Zora handled the situation. "She never made that boy feel bad about it," he explained, yet "she never made me think she was minimizing the loss."

The first issue of *Fire!!* was finally published in November 1926. Among its outstanding pieces were Zora's story "Sweat" and two Langston Hughes poems. Despite its fine writing, *Fire!!* was a financial disaster. For one thing, its one-dollar price was too steep for most Harlemites. Also, the creators of *Fire!!* stored hundreds of copies of the November issue in the basement of an apartment building in hope of selling them later. As fate would have it, a fire in the basement destroyed those remaining copies. A full year later, Zora was still trying to revive the magazine. "*Fire* has gone to ashes, but I still think the idea is good," she wrote to Alain Locke, whom she had affectionately nicknamed "Old Cabbage." Her efforts were in vain, however, and the November 1926 issue proved to be both the first and last appearance of *Fire!!*.

Some great news helped Zora get through the *Fire!!* disaster. Around the tail end of 1926 her anthropology professor, Franz Boas, called Zora into his office. "Papa Franz," as she called Dr. Boas behind his back, had arranged a much more appealing project for Zora than measuring heads on the streets of Harlem.

Recently Dr. Boas had written to Dr. Carter Woodson, an African American historian who earlier in 1926 had begun Negro History Week (now Black History Month). Boas had requested that the Association for the Study of Negro Life and History, which Woodson directed, make a large contribution for a special project to be conducted by his student, Zora Neale Hurston.

»»» Pistol-packin' Zora brought a gun along
on her 1927 Florida folklore journey.

Dr. Woodson granted $700 toward the project. The news got even better. The American Folklore Society had agreed to match Woodson's contribution. In today's money, the $1,400 Dr. Boas had obtained for Zora would amount to more than $20,000 — quite a large sum.

And what was the special project Dr. Boas expected Zora to conduct? She was to travel through the South between February and August of 1927. During those seven months she would visit black communities, where she would collect old folktales, songs, sayings, and jokes.

Zora viewed this as a wonderful opportunity to accomplish several goals at once. By collecting African American folklore, she might make a name for herself in the field of anthropology. The material she gathered might go into a book on folklore, and might even be of use to her in writing stories and plays. Besides, she still had an untapped supply of "travel dust" that made her feet itch to return to her native South. Being in a warm climate instead of frigid New York City during the winter was also a pleasant prospect.

Zora decided to begin her journey in the state she knew best. Shortly after her thirty-sixth birthday in 1927, she went by train to Jacksonville, Florida, to start a new chapter of her life.

1927

ZORA DEPARTED FOR THE SOUTH at the beginning of a memorable year for Americans. In 1927 President Calvin Coolidge announced that he wasn't running for reelection, Charles Lindbergh made the first nonstop solo airplane flight across the Atlantic Ocean, and *The Jazz Singer*, with Al Jolson, ushered in the age of "talking" pictures. It was a big year for sports, too. In 1927 "the Bambino," Babe Ruth, slammed a record sixty home runs, and Gene Tunney retained the heavyweight crown by defeating Jack Dempsey in a bout that boxing fans still argue over today.

For black southerners, the year 1927 saw the continuation of a shameful practice. The U.S. Constitution guarantees Americans the right to a fair trial. However, from time to time black people accused of wrongdoing were murdered by white mobs, often by hanging, without benefit of a trial. This practice was called lynching. Some lynching victims were accused of nothing more serious than "talking sassy to white folks." This was why Grandma Potts had worried so much about Zora asking white people for rides when she had been a child. From 1920 to 1926, more than 250 African Americans were lynched, most of them in the southern states. Before 1927 ended, sixteen more blacks would be lynched. A black woman traveling alone through remote areas of the South was in real danger of running into trouble from groups of whites. For this reason, after her arrival in Florida, Zora carried a handgun in her purse for protection.

In Jacksonville, Zora stayed at the home of her older brother John Cornelius, who operated a meat market in that city. John Cornelius advised Zora against traveling by public transportation from town to town. Bus and train seating in the South was segregated, and someone with Zora's proud temperament might very well experience difficulties. Travel about by automobile, Zora's brother advised. With John Cornelius's help, Zora spent $300 of her $1,400 on a car that she named "Sassy Susie."

»»» Zora sits on the running board of the used 1927 Nash she bought for a folklore-collecting expedition.

Zora drove Sassy Susie 135 miles to her hometown, Eatonville, which she expected would be a treasure trove of folklore. Although twenty-two years had passed since she had left home in 1905, many families Zora had known as a child still lived in the town. She was invited to stay in the home of a childhood friend, and Zora was soon frequenting Joe Clarke's store and other places in town to do her collecting.

People were cordial to her, but Zora had little success at first. In fact, during the entire seven-month period in 1927 that she traveled about trying to gather stories, songs, jokes, and sayings, she obtained little more material than what she had heard as a child at Joe Clarke's store.

The fault was all hers, Zora later admitted. With her New York clothes, newly acquired New York accent, and notebook in hand, she made people feel that she was no longer one of them. They weren't enough at ease with her to tell her what she wanted. Sometimes they weren't even sure what she was after. In her autobiography, Zora explained:

> I did not have the right approach. The glamor of Barnard College was still upon me. I dwelt in marble halls. I knew where the material was, all right. But, I went about asking, in carefully accented Barnardese, "Pardon me, but do you know any folk tales or folk songs?" The men and women who had whole treasuries of material just seeping through their pores, looked at me and shook their heads. No, they never heard of anything like that around there. Oh, I got a few little items. But compared with what I did later, not enough to make a flea a waltzing jacket.

"Papa Franz" wanted periodic reports from her, so she copied segments of her notebook and mailed them to him. On May 3, 1927, Dr. Boas criticized her with the comment: "I find that what you obtained is very largely repetition of the kind of material that has been collected so much." Zora was crushed that her anthropology professor was disappointed in her work, yet she knew that he was right.

Just sixteen days after Dr. Boas wrote that stinging note, Zora did something that surprised nearly everyone who knew her. After seven years of mostly long-distance courtship by letter, Zora and Herbert Sheen met in St. Augustine, Florida. There, the two were married on May 19, 1927. The groom was thirty years old and completing his last year at Chicago's Rush Medical College. The bride was thirty-six but probably had convinced Herbert that she was about ten years younger.

Zora was not enthusiastic about marriage. She wrote about her wedding day in her autobiography: "It was not my happiest day. I was assailed by doubts. For the first time since I met him, I asked myself if I really were in love, or if this had been a habit." Three days after her wedding, Zora informed two writer friends about her marriage. "Dear Little Sisters D & H," she began her letter to the cousins Dorothy West and Helene Johnson. "Yes, I'm married now, Mrs. Herbert Arnold Sheen, if you please." She told them that she was retaining her maiden name, then changed the subject, asking whether either of them could lend her a certain book.

Following a brief honeymoon, Zora resumed her folklore-collecting travels, with Herbert accompanying her for several days before returning to medical school in Chicago. Their marriage was a disaster. Over the next few months

Zora and Herbert saw each other sporadically before deciding to separate permanently near the end of 1927. After a few years of total separation and little
if any communication, their divorce became final in 1931.

Everyone who knew Zora or who has studied her life has wrestled with
these questions: Why did her marriage to Herbert Sheen end so quickly? Why
did she marry him in the first place if she had so little interest in being with
him? Zora never offered an explanation except to tell Langston Hughes that
being married "held back" her career. Herbert later claimed that their interests
were far too different for them to be compatible. "Zora was full of her work,
and I was full of mine," he said.

These explanations don't exactly ring true, however. After all, Zora had
had seven years to decide whether or not to marry Herbert. Not only that,
but she later married twice more, and each of those marriages also lasted less
than a year. Perhaps all we can say about Zora and marriage is that part of
her wanted to live a conventional life, but a bigger part of her rebelled against
responsibilities and needed to feel completely free to do what she wanted.

In July of 1927, Zora drove Sassy Susie to Mobile, Alabama, for what
promised to be the highlight of her folklore-collecting trip. Near Mobile lived
an elderly man who was a piece of living history. His name was Cudjo Lewis,
and he was the only remaining survivor of the *Clotilde*, which in 1859 had
delivered the last known cargo of slaves to the United States. Cudjo had been
a slave for six years until the end of the Civil War.

Interviewing a native African who had been a slave in America was an
anthropologist's dream. Cudjo, who must have been in his eighties, told Zora
about his childhood in Africa and about his people's folklore and customs. He

»»» Cudjo (Kossula) Lewis, whom Zora interviewed in Alabama, was a survivor of the *Clotilde,* the last ship to deliver a cargo of slaves to the United States. Lewis is shown with his twin great-granddaughters, Mary and Martha.

also recalled how, nearly seventy years earlier, he and others in his village had been captured, taken on the ship to America, and sold into slavery in Mobile. Zora wrote an article about him called "Cudjo's Own Story of the Last African Slaver," which she planned to send to the *Journal of Negro History*, edited by Dr. Carter Woodson. Zora was so eager to impress the man who was providing half the money for her trip that she committed the cardinal sin for an author.

There was a little-known book in the Mobile Historical Society titled *Historic Sketches of the Old South*, by Emma Langdon Roche, which contained information about Cudjo Lewis. Figuring that nobody would notice, Zora copied whole passages from Roche's book into her article with only slight changes. Of course, nonfiction authors routinely gather information from other sources, but they use several books for research and transform the material into their own words. Zora lifted page after page almost word for word out of Roche's book. In fact, Zora's article was only about 25 percent original. The other 75 percent was plagiarized, or stolen, from *Historic Sketches of the Old South*.

Dr. Woodson published Zora's article in the October 1927 issue of the *Journal of Negro History*. Miss Roche's book was so obscure that Zora's theft wasn't discovered until 1972, by which time Dr. Boas, Dr. Woodson, Zora herself, and most other people connected with her career were no longer living. Had her plagiarism been revealed back in 1927, Zora might have been expelled from Barnard College, kicked out of Columbia University's Anthropology Department, lost whatever was left of her $1,400 grant, and had her reputation as a writer so badly tarnished that publishers would be reluctant to consider her work. It was good luck on Zora's part that her foolish decision to steal material from another author wasn't discovered for forty-five years.

While traveling, Zora had written letters to Langston Hughes, trying to persuade her best friend to come down south and join her in her quest for folklore. From time to time Zora and Langston had discussed writing a "folk opera" together. It would show scenes of black life and feature songs and dancing — a little like the operettas Miss M's troupe had performed, except with African American themes and jazz and blues music. As part of her campaign to persuade Langston to join her, Zora exaggerated her accomplishments: "Getting some gorgeous material down here, verse and prose, *magnificent*. Shall save some juicy bits for you and me. Wish you could join me after school closes."

Langston, who now attended Lincoln University in Pennsylvania, had been spending his summer vacation on a southern tour of his own. In late July, just as Zora was finishing her interviews with Cudjo Lewis, Langston met her in Mobile, Alabama. He agreed to accompany Zora on the rest of her southern tour and then return north with her in Sassy Susie.

With Zora behind the wheel, the two writers toured Alabama, Georgia, and South Carolina for a few weeks, collecting folklore. As they drove from town to town and then began the long trip back to New York, they discussed the folk opera they planned to write together and caught up on news and gossip. Zora confided to Lang something that she hadn't told Dr. Franz Boas or Annie Nathan Meyer: She was married, and her husband lived halfway across the country. Langston also had a bombshell for Zora. He had found a patron—a person who provided him with funds so that he could spend his time writing.

»»» During their 1927 summer car trip from Florida to New York, Zora and Langston Hughes
lectured at Alabama's Tuskegee Institute. There they met Jessie Fauset (left),
former literary editor of the *Crisis,* which published Hughes's early poems.

When Zora asked about his patron's identity, Langston would only refer to her as "Godmother." One of Godmother's rules, he explained, was that he couldn't reveal her name. But the best news for Zora was that Langston thought Godmother would like her folklore work. Did Zora want him to help arrange for her to meet Godmother? Of course she did!

Upon their arrival back in New York City in late August 1927, Zora showed Dr. Boas the folklore material she had collected. In her autobiography, she wrote: "I stood before Papa Franz and cried salty tears. He gave me a good going over, but later I found that he was not as disappointed as he let me think."

Nonetheless, Zora believed that if she could tour the South for another year or two, she would collect much better folklore than she had the first time. Besides pleasing Dr. Boas, the new material would enhance the folk opera she and Lang planned to write together. But who would pay for another southern trip for Zora?

Thanks to Langston Hughes and Alain Locke, within a few days of her return to New York, Zora received an invitation to visit Godmother. On September 20, 1927, Zora rang the bell at Godmother's penthouse apartment at 399 Park Avenue. She was shown in to meet a seventy-three-year-old white-haired woman who would mean much to her writing career over the next few years.

That day, and in the weeks to come, Zora learned about Godmother's background. Her name was Charlotte Louise van der Veer Quick Mason— Mrs. Charlotte Mason for short. Born in Princeton, New Jersey, in 1854, she had married a wealthy physician. Mrs. Mason had a keen interest in anthropology, and, following her husband's death in 1903, she had traveled through the American West, living with Plains Indians for a time. She had become convinced that "primitives," as she called nonwhite people, had greater spirituality and a stronger feeling for the basics of life than white people. She began to use some of her wealth to help support creative artists who focused on the "primitives." She started by financing the musicologist Natalie Curtis's research into Native American songs and legends that went into Miss Curtis's *The Indians' Book*, published in 1907.

Twenty years later, Mrs. Mason had attended a lecture by Professor Alain Locke and concluded that African American creative artists were brimming over with spirituality but often needed financial help. In 1927 she began inviting black people involved in the creative arts to her elegant Park Avenue penthouse. She aided those who she felt had talent.

Alain Locke was the first African American writer she had decided to assist. In fact, Alain served as a kind of talent scout for Godmother, recommending other gifted but needy black writers, artists, and musicians. At Langston Hughes's urging, Alain Locke had brought up Zora's name to Godmother. Godmother asked Zora: What was the project for which she needed funds?

She wanted to collect black folklore in the South and then publish her findings, Zora explained. She had recently completed her first southern tour but had barely scratched the surface. The richest nuggets of songs, stories, and sayings were still waiting for her to dig them out.

Zora was so excited about her first interview with Godmother that the next day she sent Langston a note about it. "Dear Bambino," wrote Zora, "I went to see Mrs. Mason and I think we got on famously. God, I hope so!"

»»» Mrs. Charlotte Mason, or "Godmother," supported the creative endeavors
of such artists as Langston Hughes, Alain Locke, and Zora.

Over the next few weeks, Zora returned to 399 Park Avenue for more interviews. Zora knew that Godmother liked her. A big reason was that God-mother saw that Zora was true to her roots — an African American who was proud of being black. Godmother also thought that Zora's project had "soul," as she referred to ideas of which she approved. Godmother offered to pay Zora two hundred dollars a month so that she could spend 1928 collecting folklore in the South. Mrs. Mason also agreed to provide her with a car and a movie camera to help her pursue her project. In return for Mrs. Mason's support, Zora would have to obey three rules.

First, Zora must address Mrs. Mason as "Godmother." Second, Zora must keep Godmother's identity secret, for she didn't want every would-be painter, composer, or novelist camping on her doorstep, seeking money. Between 1927 and the early 1930s, Mrs. Mason gave a total of $75,000 — equal to a mil-lion dollars today — to African American creative artists, all of whom agreed to these two rules. But in Zora's case there was a third rule. All of the folklore Zora collected was to be turned over to Godmother, who retained final say about what was to be done with it.

Godmother's first two rules were fine with Zora, but the third one dis-turbed her. It meant that Godmother could decide whether Zora and Langston could use what she collected in their folk opera. It meant that Godmother could prevent Zora from showing the material to Dr. Boas. Furthermore, if she so chose, Godmother could hand over Zora's material to an established author and have him or her turn it into a book. In that case, Zora's role would be reduced to that of a researcher.

Mrs. Mason confided to Zora that she wanted to retain ownership of the material to make sure that it wouldn't be "commercialized" — turned into a cheap Hollywood movie or a sleazy magazine story about "Negro customs down south." She didn't really intend to prevent Zora from using the material in any reasonable way. Furthermore, Godmother promised Zora that if things went well, the contract would be extended through 1929. Godmother asked Zora to come to her penthouse on December 8 and sign a contract.

The decision was easy for Zora. She felt that Mrs. Mason was sincere, for her dear friend Langston Hughes had great respect for her, once calling her "an amazing, brilliant, powerful personality," adding that he "was fascinated by her, and loved her." Besides, without Godmother's assistance, Zora wouldn't be able to go on her folklore-collecting trip. There was another reason why Zora came to 399 Park Avenue to sign on the dotted line. If need be, she planned to defy the clause that granted Mrs. Mason the right to decide how the material would be used. Folklore was something that the people handed down generation after generation. It belonged to everyone, so how could anyone claim that he or she owned a folktale, saying, or song?

On December 14, 1927 — six days after signing the contract with Godmother — Zora went to New York's Penn Station and boarded a southbound train. As she headed back to Mobile, Alabama, Zora felt confident that this trip would launch her career as a folklorist and writer.

"Most Gorgeous Possibilities"

ZORA EVIDENTLY FELT GUILTY about the Cudjo Lewis episode, for the first thing she did upon arriving in Mobile was to arrange for more meetings with the elderly ex-slave. She spent much of January interviewing Lewis and was particularly moved by how, seventy years after being taken into slavery, the old man still missed his people in Africa and cried as he spoke about them. Out of respect for his roots, Zora usually called him by his African name, Kossula. A few years later she would write a book about him, *The Life of Kossula* (also called *Barracoon*), but it was never published in her lifetime.

By late January, Zora had finished her interviews with Cudjo Lewis and was ready to move on. She had sold Sassy Susie back in New York, so she now bought another car — a shiny gray Chevy — and drove it to Florida to begin what would turn out to be two straight years of collecting folklore.

One of her first stops was the town of Loughman in the woods of central Florida. There she rented a room at a boardinghouse owned by the Everglades

»»» Early in 1928, Zora lived in the "quarters" of the Everglades Cypress Lumber Company.

Cypress Lumber Company and tried to befriend the workers who cut down the trees and processed the wood in the sawmill. The men and women employed by the lumber company were a tough bunch, and at first they were wary of the stranger with the flashy car. They suspected that she might be some kind of government agent or even a private detective looking for a wrongdoer. Convincing them that she had traveled more than 1,100 miles to collect folklore would be difficult, Zora knew, so she concocted a lie to explain her appearance out of nowhere in her fancy car.

At the time, Prohibition, a period from 1920 to 1933 when alcoholic drinks were outlawed throughout the country, was in full swing. During Prohibition, bootleggers broke the law by manufacturing or smuggling alcoholic drinks into the country and selling them. Zora told the lumber workers that she was a bootlegger hiding out from government agents in Miami and Jacksonville.

The lumber workers believed Zora's tall tale and began to invite her to their "payday parties," held every other Saturday night. As she ate, drank, and danced with them, Zora was gradually accepted into the group. She had brought a guitar along on the trip, and she would sing "John Henry" or another African American folk song and then lend her guitar to anyone who wanted to sing. "Big Sweet," who was considered the lumber camp's toughest woman, especially befriended her. Big Sweet enjoyed riding around in Zora's car, and promised Zora that she would "do [her] fighting for [her]" if anyone started trouble with her.

»»» These lumbermen were returning from a day's work in the cypress mill.

After a while, Zora confided the truth to Big Sweet: She had come to Loughman to collect "lies" and old songs and sayings. With Big Sweet's help, Zora put up signs at the post office and the lumber camp store. On a certain date there was to be a "lying contest," with cash awards given out for the four best "lies."

On contest day, there was a big turnout. To make sure there would be no arguing over who was worthy of the prizes, Zora appointed Big Sweet as the judge. The event was so successful that Zora held another lying contest a week or so later.

"I believe I have almost as many stories now as I got on my entire trip last year," she wrote to Langston Hughes. Regarding their folk opera, she added, "Langston, Langston, this is going to be *big*. Most gorgeous possibilities are showing themselves constantly."

Several people who were too shy to enter the lying contests visited Zora privately to tell her a story or joke, or to sing a song that had been handed down in their family since slavery days. This nearly cost Zora her life.

Zora became friendly with a lumber worker called Slim who was a storehouse of old folktales. She let Slim ride in her car and spent a lot of time writing down his "lies." Zora's friendliness with Slim angered a woman named Lucy who had once been his girlfriend and who hoped to win him back. Lucy grew so jealous of Zora that at the next "payday party" she rushed at Zora with a knife, attempting to stab her.

Zora either didn't have her handgun with her or she was too terrified to find it. Later she wrote about this incident: "I saw sudden death very near. I was paralyzed with fear." Fortunately, before Lucy could stab Zora, Big Sweet appeared. She dove at Lucy and began fighting her, yelling for Zora to get out of there. "I ran to my room, threw my things in the car and left the place," Zora wrote in her autobiography. "When the sun came up I was a hundred miles up the road, headed for New Orleans."

On the way to New Orleans, Zora stopped in the community of Magazine, Alabama, where she held more lying contests. From there she drove to some undisclosed location on Alabama's Tombigbee River to interview an ex-slave woman who was "older than Cudjo" and "a better talker," as she confided to Langston Hughes. By early August she had arrived in New Orleans, where she learned about voodoo and the nineteenth-century "voodoo priestess" Marie Leveau.

Voodoo, also known as hoodoo, is a set of beliefs that scholars trace to traditional African religious practices. Followers of voodoo claim that through magic spells and help from the spirit world, people can control various aspects of their lives such as curing illnesses, sparking romances, and placing curses on enemies. Although New Orleans had been home to many voodoo practitioners, the most famous was the legendary Marie Leveau. Among her supernatural abilities, Leveau could supposedly rise out of Lake Pontchartrain holding burning candles and then walk on top of the water to shore. Such stories fascinated Zora, who as a child had told her mother that she had walked on a lake and spoken with the fish. Zora decided to do an in-depth study of voodoo in New Orleans.

Few anthropologists would have attempted what Zora did. Instead of studying voodoo as an outsider, she apprenticed herself to a series of the city's best-known voodoo priests and priestesses over a period of several months.

One of her teachers was Luke Turner, who was reputedly Marie Leveau's grandnephew. Turner put Zora through a ritual for which she had to lie, silent and alone, on a couch for three days and three nights. All that time she was forbidden food, but she was allowed to drink water from a pitcher.

"On the third night, I had dreams that seemed real," she later wrote. "In one, I strode across the heavens with lightning flashing from under my feet, and grumbling thunder following in my wake." Luke Turner gave her some instructions based on these dreams: "I was to walk with the storm, and get my answers to life in storms." Turner also gave Zora her voodoo name, the Rain-Bringer, and painted a yellow and red lightning bolt on her back as her special symbol.

At the end of 1928, Zora returned to New York for a visit. Godmother was so pleased with the material Zora had collected that she renewed her contract for another year. Godmother would continue her financial support for Zora for a total of nearly five years.

The new year, 1929, brought two close calls for Zora. In July, while collecting folklore in St. Augustine, Florida, she suffered terrible abdominal pains. She knew the problem couldn't be her appendix, for it had been removed more than ten years earlier when she had vowed to "find the road that [she] must follow" if she survived. She rushed to a hospital in St. Augustine, where doctors concluded that something was wrong with her liver, an extremely vital organ. Either the doctors were mistaken or Zora had amazing recuperative powers, for after only a few days she was out of the hospital and back on the road. She temporarily kicked off the travel dust, however, and decided to spend all of August and September in Miami, Florida.

While a stenographer typed her folklore notes, Zora began a forbidden project. Without asking Godmother's permission, Zora used some of her collected material to start writing the folk opera she and Langston Hughes had planned to do together. By August 17 she had completed seven skits, and she wrote Langston, "I am now writing music, and if I do say so I have one or two snappy airs." When two authors collaborate on a project, they usually divide up the work to make the most of their talents. Zora and Langston may have decided that she would write the rough draft and he would do much of the rewriting and polishing. Or perhaps Zora was so eager that she just went ahead and began their folk opera on her own.

While in Miami, Zora saw a performance by some dancers from the Bahamas. "I just had to know more," she wrote in her autobiography. "So without giving Godmother a chance to object, I sailed for Nassau," the island country's capital.

After arriving in the Bahamas, Zora collected folk songs, took movies of Bahamian dancers with the camera Godmother had bought for her, and learned to do the native dances herself. She also had another brush with death. In late September a powerful hurricane struck the Bahamas. Its winds, which reached 150 miles per hour, blew down more than three hundred homes in Nassau, including the house where Zora was staying with a Bahamian family. On this occasion, Zora truly did get her "answers to life in storms," for she had a feeling of impending doom and led everyone out of the house before the wind destroyed it. Years later, Zora's hurricane experience in the Bahamas would inspire a memorable scene in her most famous book, *Their Eyes Were Watching God*.

In letters to Langston Hughes, her best friend, Zora related the details about the hurricane and the highlights of the places she visited. She confessed to Lang that when she left Nassau to return to Florida, she had "only [her] return ticket and 24 cents." At the end of the same letter she told him, "You are my mainstay in all crises. No matter what may happen, I feel you can fix it."

Two months later, while back in New Orleans, she wrote, "Well, I tell you, Langston, I am nothing without you." Around New Year's Day of 1930, while on a return trip to the Bahamas, she closed a postcard to Langston with

»»» Zora made two trips to the Bahamas.

the words, "See you soon, Love & everything." Zora Neale Hurston and Langston Hughes seemed to have forged a friendship that would last a lifetime. Who could have guessed that in a few months they would be engaged in one of the fiercest literary battles of the century?

"You, LANGSTON HUGHES, Cut Me to the Quick"

ZORA ARRIVED IN NEW YORK in March 1930 with two manuscripts in hand. One was the rough draft of the folklore project for which she had been collecting material for more than two years. It would eventually appear as *Mules and Men*, but more than five years would pass before a publisher would accept and print the book. The other manuscript was the beginning of the folk opera Zora intended to co-write with Langston Hughes. This project would bring misery to just about everyone connected with it.

Soon after Zora's return, Godmother informed her that she didn't want her living in the big city. New York offered too many distractions for Zora to do her best at revising the folklore manuscript. Instead, Godmother rented an apartment for Zora twenty-five miles from New York in Westfield, New Jersey. Zora was pleased, for she would be living just a few doors from Langston Hughes, whom Godmother had already established in an apartment there.

Godmother had more good news for Zora. She had hired a secretary to type manuscripts for Langston, who was finishing his first novel, *Not Without Laughter*. The secretary, Louise Thompson, was a bright young woman who had formerly taught at Hampton Institute, an African American college in Virginia. Now that Zora was moving to Westfield, Miss Thompson was to split her time doing work for both writers.

At first, the arrangement in Westfield worked beautifully. Langston, Zora, and Louise liked one another and were together much of the day. Langston helped Zora edit her folklore manuscript, and Louise worked late into the night typing the daily revisions. Lang and Zora also found time to work together on their secret project, which had undergone a big change.

Langston told Zora that, while talking to theater people, he had been advised that what was needed was a comedy about African Americans. He had become convinced that a play about the humor in black life had a good chance of becoming a Broadway hit and perhaps even a Hollywood movie. Although she had put in many hours writing skits and music for the folk opera they had planned, Zora was tempted by the prospect of a big hit. She agreed to discard the folk opera idea and start over from scratch on the comedy.

The two writers decided to base their comedy on Zora's story "The Bone of Contention." Set in Eatonville, the story involves two hunters who shoot at a wild turkey at the same moment and then argue over who killed the bird. The dispute becomes so heated that one man picks up a bone from a dead mule and uses it to knock the other man unconscious, leading to his arrest and trial for assault and battery. The story includes a lot of amusing events as the townspeople side with one or the other of the hunters.

Zora and Langston created most of their play in Westfield between March and June 1930. They named it *Mule Bone: A Comedy of Negro Life.* As they composed, they dictated to Louise, who typed it up. Since Zora and Langston didn't want Godmother to know about their play, Louise was not paid by Mrs. Mason for typing *Mule Bone.* Instead, the two coauthors agreed to pay Louise to type their project — which didn't remain secret for long.

Somehow Godmother found out that instead of devoting all their time to their serious writing, Zora and Langston were working on a slapstick comedy. Possibly she was informed of this by Alain Locke, who helped Godmother keep tabs on Langston's and Zora's activities. Godmother was furious. She felt that a Broadway and Hollywood slapstick comedy was a waste of her "godchildren's" talents. It was just the kind of thing she *didn't* want them to do.

There was another reason for Godmother's anger. Had they spoken with her about wanting to work on a comedy together, she might have reluctantly given Zora and Langston her blessing to go ahead and have a little fun. But instead of discussing it, they had tried to keep it a secret from her.

Mrs. Mason has been sharply criticized for exerting too much control over Zora and Langston. After all, to grow as artists, writers need to experiment and sometimes even fail. In Godmother's defense, though, Zora and Langston had signed contracts and were being paid by her to do certain work. Besides, Mrs. Mason knew that one of the pitfalls writers face is drifting from project to project without completing any of them properly. She was trying to keep them focused on the work at hand: Langston on the forthcoming publication of *Not Without Laughter* and Zora on whipping her folklore material into shape so that it might become a book.

Zora and Langston tried their best to patch things up with Mrs. Mason. They visited her, and meekly asked permission to spend some of their time on *Mule Bone*. Godmother reluctantly gave her consent. While privately referring to Godmother as the "Park Avenue dragon," Zora also wrote notes to her, trying to get back in Mrs. Mason's good graces. For example, on May 18, 1930 — Godmother's seventy-sixth birthday — Zora wrote her a letter dripping with honey:

> *Darling my God-Flower,*
> *Spring means birth, but the real upspringing of life comes on May*
> *18, when you renew your promise to the world to shine for another*
> *year. You are God's flower and my flower and Langston's flower*
> *and the world's blossom.*
>
> *I really should not extend my congratulations to you on this*
> *day, but to all those who have been fortunate enough to touch you.*
> *It is you who give out life and light and we who receive. May I*
> *be spared for a long long time so that I may throw back a bit of*
> *the radiance you shed on me. My most pure and uprushing love,*
> *darling flower.*
>
>

Most devotedly,
Zora

Mrs. Mason may have gagged on all the sugar in this note. Yet something about Zora appealed to Godmother, and she kept her on her payroll for two more years. Langston Hughes and Louise Thompson would suffer a quite different fate at the hands of Godmother.

More trouble about *Mule Bone* was on the way. Despite their allowances from Godmother, Zora and Langston were barely scraping by financially and couldn't afford to pay Louise for typing their play. Without first clearing it with Zora, Langston worked out a deal with Louise. Instead of paying her a few dollars per day for typing, they would later split the profits earned by *Mule Bone* three ways. Besides giving Louise a one-third interest in *Mule Bone*, Langston offered her the job of business manager if and when the play opened on Broadway.

When she learned about the agreement made privately between Langston and Louise, Zora flew into a rage that dwarfed Godmother's explosion. She was fond of Louise, Zora told Langston, but who ever heard of a typist getting a one-third interest in a play?

In all probability, Louise, who was a former college teacher, made suggestions and corrections that improved *Mule Bone* as she typed it. But Zora was right. It was extremely unusual to offer the typist a third of the profits from a play. Still, the extent of Zora's anger shocked Langston, who had simply thought that offering Louise a piece of the action was a nice way to include a friend in their venture while settling their debt to her.

Several explanations have been offered for Zora's wrath. Perhaps she was counting on the profits from *Mule Bone* as her ticket to independence from Godmother. Perhaps what galled her was that the deal had been made behind her back — much like Godmother's reaction when she learned that Zora and Langston had been writing their comedy without telling her. It has been suggested that Zora secretly had a crush on Langston and became jealous of the attention he was heaping on Louise. The likeliest explanation is that Zora had looked forward to collaborating with Langston for years, and felt hurt and resentful that he was treating Louise as an equal partner. In any case, Zora and Langston's friendship seriously deteriorated around mid-1930 because of their disagreement over Louise's role in *Mule Bone*.

The summer of 1930 should have been a joyous time for Langston Hughes, whose first novel was published in July. But it proved to be one of the most miserable summers of his life. Just before *Not Without Laughter* came off the presses, Godmother told him some bad news. The Great Depression was under way, a period of hard times that among other things helped end the Harlem Renaissance. Like millions of other Americans, Godmother had less money than before. She informed Langston that she could no longer support some of her "godchildren," including him. When the stroke of midnight came, Langston begged Godmother to keep him on her payroll, sending her notes with pleas such as "I love you, Godmother. I need you." But Godmother was finished helping Langston Hughes — perhaps placing most of the blame on him for the entire *Mule Bone* mess. Not long afterward, Mrs. Mason also removed Louise Thompson from her payroll.

Langston felt so depressed about all that had happened between Godmother, Zora, and him that he became ill, complaining of nausea and other maladies. To recover, he returned to Cleveland for a while to live with his mother. Zora, too, was distraught about what had happened and escaped the situation by leaving Westfield, New Jersey, and returning to New York City to live. She confessed to a friend that she often awoke in the middle of the night crying over the loss of her friendship with Langston Hughes.

Over the next few months, Zora and Langston had opportunities to patch up their quarrel. But that didn't come to pass — largely because each expected

CHARACTERS

JIM WESTON: Guitarist, Methodist, slightly arrogant, agressive, some-
                        what self-important, ready with his tongue.

DAVE CARTER: Dancer, Baptist, soft, happy-go-lucky character, slightly
                        dumb and unable to talk rapidly and wittily.

DAISY TAYLOR: Methodist, domestic servant, plump, dark and sexy, self-
                        conscious of clothes and appeal, fickle.

JOE CLARK: The Mayor, storekeeper and postmaster, arrogant, ignorant
                        and powerful in a self-assertive way, large, fat man,
                        Methodist.

ELDER SIMMS: Methodist minister, newcomer in town, ambitious, small and
                        fly, but not very intelligent.

ELDER CHILDERS: Big, loose-jointed, slow spoken but not dumb. Long resident
                        in the town, calm and sure of himself.

KATIE CARTER: Dave's aunt, little old wizened dried-up lady.

MRS. MATTIE CLARK: The Mayor's wife, fat and flabby mulatto high-pitched voice.

THE MRS. REV. SIMMS: Large and agressive.

THE MRS. REV. CHILDERS: Just a wife who thinks of details.

LUM BOGER: Young town marshall about twenty, tall, gangly, with big
                        flat feet, liked to show off in public.

TEET MILLER: Village vamp who is jealous of DAISY.

LIGE MOSELY: A village wag.

WALTER THOMAS: Another village wag.

ADA LEWIS: A promiscuous lover.

DELLA LEWIS: Baptist, poor housekeeper, mother of ADA.

BOOTSIE PITTS: A local vamp.

MRS. DILCIE ANDERSON: Village housewife, Methodist.

WILLIE NIXON: Methodist, short runt.

»»» Zora submitted her play *Mule Bone* to the Library of Congress in order to
establish her copyright. Here we have the cast of characters in her drama.

the other to take responsibility for what had happened. The result was that their feud only deepened.

Zora felt that *Mule Bone* was mostly hers, for its plot was based on her story, its setting was her hometown of Eatonville, and she had done most of the writing. By the fall of 1931, Zora had rewritten the play, removing or revising Langston's contributions. She now was convinced that *Mule Bone* was solely her work.

In September, Langston phoned Zora with some news that he hoped would bring them together. He had shown *Mule Bone* to Jasper Deeter, the founder and artistic director of the Hedgerow Theatre outside Philadelphia. Mr. Deeter was fascinated by the play and wanted to stage it at Hedgerow. The only problem was, act 2 needed reworking. Could Zora send along any rewrites she had done to that part?

Zora was flabbergasted. Didn't Langston realize that his making promises to Louise Thompson without first consulting her had led to their split? Now he had shown the old version of the play to a theatrical executive, again without asking her. She had completely rewritten *Mule Bone*, all of which was now her property, she angrily informed Langston. Zora's response wounded Langston, who had hoped she would be grateful that he had found a producer for the play. He also resented her claiming sole ownership of *their* play, for which he claimed that he had done a third of the work. If *Mule Bone* was ever performed with only Zora's name as author, he threatened, he would sue her. Not wanting to be part of a legal battle over the authorship of *Mule Bone*, the Hedgerow Theatre lost interest in the play.

A few months later, an odd series of events involving *Mule Bone* occurred. Zora and Langston had a mutual friend, Carl Van Vechten, whom she had met at the *Opportunity* awards banquet back in 1925. Zora showed her *Mule Bone* rewrite to Carl, who, without telling her, forwarded the play to a friend in the theater. The play was passed on to Rowena and Russell Jelliffe, a couple who ran the Karamu Theatre in Cleveland, Ohio. The Jelliffes loved *Mule Bone* and decided to present it at Karamu.

One day Langston Hughes, who was still staying at his mother's home in Cleveland, dropped by the Karamu Theatre to visit his friends the Jelliffes. Rowena and Russell mentioned that in February 1931 they planned to stage *Mule Bone*, a play by someone named Zora Neale Hurston. Now it was Langston's turn to feel that Zora had sneaked behind his back. He wrote to Zora demanding to know why she had sent their play, with only her name on it, to the Jelliffes. Zora responded that she too was mystified as to how a copy of her *Mule Bone* rewrite had wound up in the Jelliffes' hands.

A flurry of letters, telegrams, and phone calls among Zora, Langston, Carl Van Vechten, and the Jelliffes made it clear that Zora had not sent the play to Karamu. As they communicated, Zora and Langston seemed to be putting their dispute behind them. For example, on January 18, 1931, Zora confessed how she had felt about his offering Louise a one-third interest in the play: "I was just plain hurt. You, LANGSTON HUGHES, cut me to the quick." When Zora decided to visit Cleveland in early February to work out a deal with the Jelliffes and revise the play with Langston, it appeared that their feud would soon be over.

»»» Photographer Carl Van Vechten created portraits of Harlem Renaissance actors, artists, and writers. He and Hurston became close friends. "Zora," he wrote, "is picturesque, witty, electric, indiscreet, and unreliable."

Not long before Zora went to Cleveland, she received a letter from Langston that apparently had been delayed in the mail. Written at the height of his anger over the Karamu incident, it contained threats of a lawsuit against Zora. The upshot was, by the time she had completed the five-hundred-mile drive to Cleveland, Zora was once again ready to erupt.

On the afternoon of February 3, 1931 — a day after her arrival — Zora met with Rowena Jelliffe and Langston Hughes at the home of Langston's mother,

Carrie Clark. Langston, who was now suffering from severe throat troubles in addition to his other health problems, remained in bed during the conference. It wasn't much of a conference, for Zora did most of the talking. According to Langston Hughes, "[Zora] pushed her hat back, ground her teeth, and shook manuscripts in my face." Zora denounced Langston and the Jelliffes for trying to steal her play, and was so insulting that she pushed Mrs. Clark past her limit: Hughes later explained, "I had to get up out of bed to restrain my mother."

That evening, before leaving Cleveland, Zora sent a telegram to Mrs. Mason proclaiming victory over those who had tried to steal her play:

DARLING GODMOTHER
PLAY STOPPED. I SMASHED THEM ALL. BE HOME BY
WEEK END. ALL MY LOVE.
                    ZORA

The February 3 "conference" was a crucial event in Zora's life in several ways. First, it marked the end of any attempt at reconciliation between Zora and Langston. After March 1931, Zora never even wrote a single letter to Langston Hughes. Second, the breakup of the Hurston-Hughes writing team marked the end of *Mule Bone*'s chances for success. Working together, Zora and Langston might have created a hit. But Langston had nothing more to do with the play after the February 3 meeting, and the version of *Mule Bone* Zora wrote on her own was never performed anywhere in her lifetime.

A bright spot of the *Mule Bone* fiasco was that it brought Zora and Godmother closer together. Mrs. Mason had suspected that *Mule Bone* would bring disappointment to Zora and Langston, and events had proved her right. After Zora's final break with Langston, she began to show true affection toward the woman who was financing her writing career. On July 23, 1931, Zora sent a poem she had written to Mrs. Mason:

> *Godmother, for love, I thank you*
> *For kindnesses and love I thank you*
> *For Courtesy that passes earthy bounds*
> *I thank you*
> *For the giving of light that I might*
> *see beauty, I thank you*
> *For extending your arms, for the thrusting*
> *forth of your hands*
> *That roll back the uttermost horizons*
> *and extend the living world, I thank*
> *you.*

There was one more way that the *Mule Bone* episode shaped Zora as a person. Scholars still argue as to who was most at fault in her rift with Langston Hughes. But everyone agrees that Zora showed a lot of nerve to tangle with Hughes at a point when she was yet to have a major success and he was becoming a well-known author. For the rest of her life, Zora would never hesitate to stand up for herself when she thought she was being treated unfairly.

"It Cost $1.83 to Mail, and I Did Not Have It"

AT THE TIME of her final break with Langston Hughes, Zora had turned forty years old. As an author, she was known to very few readers. Her published work consisted of only about twenty stories and articles, which had appeared for the most part in small, black-oriented periodicals. She didn't yet have any books published. Perhaps the most impressive aspect of her résumé was her growing list of rejections.

She had written a book-length manuscript about Cudjo Lewis, which she called *Barracoon* and also *The Life of Kossula*, but it had been rejected. That may have actually been fortunate, for publication of her book could have brought to light the fact that she had largely plagiarized her article about Cudjo for the *Journal of Negro History*. Zora had also written a book about voodoo, but it too had been rejected. She had a preliminary draft for her book of folklore *Mules and Men*, but she was slow about editing it. Her best chance for success had been *Mule Bone*, which two theaters had wanted to present. But of course that hadn't happened because of her quarrel with Langston Hughes.

More disappointments were to come, partly because Zora still believed she would make a name for herself in the theater. In 1931 she wrote scripts for three theatrical productions, all of which were flops in one way or another.

Revues were popular in the 1930s. These productions consisted of a series of skits, dances, and songs about a particular subject or theme. First, Zora wrote skits for an African American revue called *Fast and Furious*. Zora had high hopes when it opened on Broadway on September 15, 1931, especially since the producer had told her she could expect to earn at least five hundred dollars from the production. Although the *New York Times* praised a skit Zora had written as "genuine entertainment," the critics panned the revue as a whole, calling it "mediocre" and "tiresome." *Fast and Furious* closed after just one week, and instead of five hundred, Zora received only seventy-five dollars.

Next she wrote another African American revue — which made *Fast and Furious* look like a smash hit. Called *Jungle Scandals*, it was canceled before even a single performance.

Still hopeful that success was just around the corner, Zora put together *The Great Day*, a musical that told the story of a day's events among Florida laborers. Zora rented a theater and borrowed several hundred dollars from Godmother to pay for costumes and salaries for her performers. *The Great Day* opened on January 10, 1932, at New York's John Golden Theatre. Although the critics loved it, *The Great Day* was a box-office failure and closed after just one performance. Zora wound up owing Godmother, who had bankrolled almost the entire project, a total of $611.

Zora had now written two revues and a musical over a period of half a year, and all she had to show for it financially was a large debt. She was discouraged but not beaten. "I firmly believe that I shall succeed as a writer," she declared in a letter to Godmother, who, due to the Depression, considered ending Zora's allowance. Zora began making plans to set up a food catering business to earn a living. She even informed Godmother that she intended to become "New York's Chicken Specialist"—selling chicken salad, fried chicken, and chicken soup for parties. Fortunately Mrs. Mason continued Zora's allowance—although she reduced it to one hundred and later fifty dollars a month—so she did not become New York's chicken queen after all. However, Mrs. Mason explained that she could only afford to support Zora for a few more months.

In the spring of 1932, Zora announced to Godmother that she wanted to return to Eatonville to live. She felt she could do a better job of rewriting her folklore book *Mules and Men* in her hometown. Besides, she could live more cheaply there than she could in New York City. Godmother bought Zora a train ticket and apparently forgave her $611 debt. Around May 1, Zora boarded a train in New York City and headed toward the town of her roots.

Once in Eatonville, Zora felt revived almost instantly. For some time, she had been suffering stomach trouble, but after moving into the home of a childhood friend, she informed Godmother, "My work is coming on most satisfactorily and I feel fine." Every day she arose before sunrise to work in her vegetable garden, and afterward she put in long days writing.

Working steadily, Zora needed just a few months to rewrite and polish *Mules and Men.* By the fall of 1932 the manuscript was basically complete.

After nearly five years of supporting her, Godmother now felt that Zora was ready to stand on her own. She sent her a final fifty dollars in October and then withdrew her financial support. Unlike Langston Hughes, Zora did not panic when the checks stopped arriving from 399 Park Avenue. On the contrary, Zora felt exhilarated to be completely independent at long last. Her garden, and those of her friends, supplied her with food, and her expenses in Eatonville were so small that she felt she could scrape by.

While searching for a publisher for *Mules and Men*, Zora pursued other projects. Near Eatonville in the wealthy white community of Winter Park, there was a fine school called Rollins College. Zora arranged for the college's theater director, Robert Wunsch, to stage *The Great Day* there. She rewrote the musical, retitled it *From Sun to Sun*, and recruited many of her Eatonville friends and neighbors to act in it. In January 1933 the show was performed at Rollins College and was a big hit. Zora was disappointed in one way, however. Like other southern schools, Rollins College practiced segregation. Only white people were allowed to attend the performance in the college's 1,800-seat auditorium — even though *From Sun to Sun* had been written by a black author and featured a black cast acting in a story about African Americans.

Segregation was also the rule when Zora and her troupe were invited to perform *From Sun to Sun* in several other Florida towns. In a letter to God-mother, Zora explained that she had found a way for black people to see her show, too: "Early in Feb. we sing at Hungerford, the Negro school so that our own people may hear us." The Hungerford performance meant a lot to Zora, who had attended the Eatonville school thirty-five years earlier.

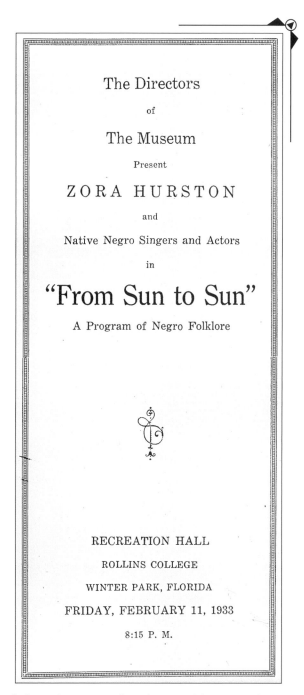

The Directors

of

The Museum

Present

ZORA HURSTON

and

Native Negro Singers and Actors

in

"From Sun to Sun"

A Program of Negro Folklore

RECREATION HALL

ROLLINS COLLEGE

WINTER PARK, FLORIDA

FRIDAY, FEBRUARY 11, 1933

8:15 P. M.

»»» Black people were not allowed to attend the 1933 performance of Zora's play *From Sun to Sun* at Rollins College in Winter Park, Florida.

Meanwhile, Zora had written a short story that she had been thinking about for four years. Called "The Gilded Six-Bits," it was a love story about a married couple in Eatonville. Zora showed it to Robert Wunsch, the Rollins College theater director who had helped her stage *From Sun to Sun*. Professor Wunsch was captivated by "The Gilded Six-Bits." He read it aloud to his creative writing class and also mailed a copy to Martha Foley and Whit Burnett, a married couple who edited *Story* magazine. Foley and Burnett also liked it and sent Zora twenty dollars (equal to about three hundred dollars in today's money) as payment to publish it. When it appeared in the August 1933 issue of *Story*, "The Gilded Six-Bits" became the first story or article Zora had published in nearly two years.

Story was a prestigious magazine, and editors at major book publishing houses combed its pages searching for new talent. The first copies of the August issue were barely off the presses when Zora received letters from four publishers asking whether she had a novel they might consider. For years, Zora had mostly experienced disappointment and rejection as a writer. Now, thanks to a gem of a magazine story, publishers were courting *her*.

There was one big problem, though. Not only had Zora not completed a novel, but she hadn't even started one—"not the first word," she admitted in her autobiography. However, she wasn't about to let *that* stop her. The letter that most appealed to her was from Bertram Lippincott, head of one of the country's leading publishers, the J. B. Lippincott Company of Philadelphia. Zora wrote back saying that she was in the midst of writing a novel, which was *almost* true, for an idea for a novel had been swimming around in her head for a long time.

A few days after she answered Mr. Lippincott's letter, Zora moved a short way from Eatonville to Sanford, Florida, where nothing would distract her from writing her novel. For $1.50 a week she rented a small house where she didn't do much except write, eat, and sleep. After two weeks her money ran out and she had to regularly borrow fifty cents a week from a cousin just to buy weekly groceries. Her writing output was remarkable, though, and in only three months she had completed her novel, which she called *Jonah's Gourd Vine*. Authors generally do their best when writing about what they know. Zora's first novel was about a subject close to her heart: her parents' marriage. The novel's two main characters — John and Lucy — have the same names as her parents. There is even a deathbed scene modeled after the real-life instance when her mother asked Zora to stop the neighbors from removing the pillow from under her head.

By early October 1933, her manuscript was finished and typed. However, when Zora took it to the office of an express mail company, she found that she did not have enough money to ship the manuscript to the Lippincott Company. "It cost $1.83 to mail, and I did not have it," she wrote in her autobiography. She borrowed two dollars from an acquaintance, and on October 3 she sent off her novel.

Zora had found the town of Sanford so conducive to writing that she decided to stay there while awaiting Mr. Lippincott's decision on *Jonah's Gourd Vine*. Besides, she had a one-day job coming up in Sanford. The Seminole County Chamber of Commerce offered her twenty-five dollars to assemble part of her *From Sun to Sun* cast and perform the musical from a moving truck with a loudspeaker system. That way everyone in the town could enjoy the music. The date

»»» This photo of Zora was taken in 1935 during the
Lomax-Hurston-Barnicle folklore-collecting expedition in Florida.

chosen for the mobile performance was October 16 — a day that turned out to
be one of the most important in Zora's life.

Early on that Monday morning, the woman who owned the house Zora
was renting knocked on the door and demanded that she pay eighteen dollars in back rent that she owed. She didn't have the money just yet, Zora
explained, but she would be able to pay her debt late that afternoon after she
received the twenty-five dollars for her performance. Saying that she doubted
Zora would *ever* have as much as twenty-five dollars, the landlady ordered her
to leave the house immediately. Zora grabbed her clothes and her few other

belongings and found shelter in the home of her uncle, the Reverend Isaiah Hurston, who also lived in Sanford.

At eleven a.m., Zora and her cast climbed onto the sound truck and for the next few hours were driven through the streets of Sanford as they performed portions of *From Sun to Sun*. Sometime in the afternoon a Western Union messenger tracked down Zora on the sound truck and handed her a telegram, which she put away for safekeeping. At three p.m., Zora and her cast completed their musical tour and were paid by the Chamber of Commerce as promised. They were also presented with gift certificates allowing them to receive a certain amount of free merchandise from various stores in Sanford.

»»» Alan Lomax photographed Zora Neale Hurston, Rochelle French, and guitarist Gabriel Brown in Zora's hometown of Eatonville, Florida, during their 1935 expedition.

Zora needed shoes, so she took her gift certificate to a shoe store. She was trying on a pair of shoes when she suddenly remembered the telegram. In her autobiography she described the great moments that followed:

> When I opened it and read that Jonah's Gourd Vine was
> accepted and that Lippinicott was offering me a $200 advance,
> I tore out of that place with one old shoe and one new one on,
> and ran to the Western Union office. Lippincott had asked for an
> answer by wire and they got it! *TERMS ACCEPTED.*

"I never expect to have a greater thrill than that wire gave me," added Zora, for, to an author, few events in life are as exciting as the first acceptance of a book for publication. The two-hundred-dollar advance — money paid up front before publication — also meant a great deal to Zora, for it lifted her out of poverty, at least for the time being.

Her writer friends had undoubtedly encouraged Zora with the old saying "Once your first book is accepted, the others will be easier to sell." This was certainly true for Zora. She sent her folklore book *Mules and Men* to the Lippincott Company, which accepted it within a few months of buying *Jonah's Gourd Vine*. This meant that, after years of rejections, Zora suddenly had two books pending. That number quickly jumped to five, for Bertram Lippincott was so enthralled by her writing that he sent Zora a contract for her next three books even though she hadn't started any of them yet.

The Lippincott editors decided that *Jonah's Gourd Vine* was in good shape and scheduled it for publication in May 1934. But they thought that *Mules and Men* read too much like a textbook and needed rewriting. Having

»»» Zora posed for this photo at the 1937 *New York Times* Book Fair.

already devoted seven years to researching, writing, and revising *Mules and Men*, Zora spent a few more months in a cottage near Sanford, livening up the manuscript.

In the months before *Jonah's Gourd Vine* was to be published, Zora began to worry. What if her first novel received a poor reception? That was a real possibility, especially since she already had two strikes against her: She was black and female. At the time, most American authors were white males. Of the tiny percentage who were black, nearly all were men. A black woman author was so rare that Zora was afraid she would be treated like a circus sideshow.

To help her chances of being taken seriously, Zora asked her friend, the famous author Fannie Hurst, to write an introduction to *Jonah's Gourd Vine*. Miss Hurst did so, but in her preface she made a sly joke at Zora's expense. "A brilliant spade has turned over rich new earth," Miss Hurst wrote. "Spade" is a derogatory name for a black person, so Hurst was poking fun at Zora's race. If one of her best white friends made a cruel joke about her being black, what could Zora expect from the critics? Zora was so nervous about how *Jonah's Gourd Vine* would be received that just a week before its publication she confessed to Carl Van Vechten that she was "scared to <u>death</u> of reviews."

Zora needn't have worried, for when *Jonah's Gourd Vine* appeared in May it received glowing reviews. The *New York Times Book Review* called the book "the most vital and original novel about the American Negro that has yet been written by a member of the Negro race." When her folklore book *Mules and Men* appeared in October 1935, it too received fine reviews.

With both a fiction and a nonfiction book to her credit, Zora Neale Hurston had emerged as a new voice in American literature.

10

"I Wrote It in Seven Weeks": *Their Eyes Were Watching God*

ALTHOUGH PLENTY OF PRAISE was heaped on Zora for her first two books, neither fame nor fortune accompanied it. In all, her advances for signing to do her first five books with Lippincott probably totaled only about a thousand dollars. While the money enabled her to buy a car and pay her debts, it wasn't enough to keep her going for long. Furthermore, during her entire writing career none of her books sold more than a few thousand copies. This meant that her royalties (her share of the proceeds from the sale of her books) were typically only a few hundred dollars per year. For Zora to keep writing, she would need additional sources of income.

During the mid-1930s, Zora earned a little money by writing magazine articles and stories. In 1934 she wrote an article for the *American Mercury* titled "You Don't Know Us Negroes" that lambasted white authors who wrote about black people without knowing what they were really like. The article would have been one of the most controversial pieces Zora ever published, but the *American Mercury* chose not to print it—perhaps because the magazine's white readers would have found it insulting. But Zora was just as likely to criticize black people as white. On December 29, 1934, the *Washington Tribune* ran her article "Race Cannot Become Great Until It Recognizes Its Talent." In it she upbraided black people for failing to take pride in their own culture.

For a few months in 1934 Zora taught drama at Bethune-Cookman College, a black school in Daytona Beach, Florida. That job didn't last long, mainly because Zora clashed with Mary McLeod Bethune, who had founded the school in 1904 and who was widely considered to be the nation's foremost black woman. Mrs. Bethune assigned Zora the job of presenting a pageant to celebrate her school's thirtieth anniversary. Instead of allowing Zora to create the pageant herself, however, Mrs. Bethune handed her a script written by another faculty member. Zora thought the script was terrible—embarrassingly so.

Not only that, but Mrs. Bethune allowed other members of the faculty to help Zora direct the pageant. "One day eight people were trying to direct one scene at the same time," Zora explained in a letter. "Anyway the performance was just some students stumbling around on the stage." Because of incidents like this, Zora soon quit the Bethune-Cookman faculty.

In the fall of 1934, Zora was offered five hundred dollars by a group in Chicago to present *Singing Steel,* a new folk concert she had written that was based on her earlier musicals *The Great Day* and *From Sun to Sun.* Zora drove to the Windy City, where she stayed in a YWCA. She not only saved money by living at the Y, but recruited people she met there to sing and dance in her show. While rehearsing the show, Zora also found time to speak before women's clubs and at a Chicago bookstore about her work. Then on November 23 and 24, Zora presented *Singing Steel* at a large Chicago theater.

The audience for *Singing Steel* included some officials from the Julius Rosenwald Fund, which granted money for worthy projects. These officials thought that Zora's folklore work deserved support, and they encouraged her to apply for a Rosenwald grant to study for her doctorate in anthropology at New York's Columbia University. Becoming *Dr.* Hurston would help her gain wider acceptance as a writer, Zora believed, and in December she applied for and was promised a $3,000 grant to study for her doctorate at Columbia. This was truly a huge sum—equal to about $45,000 in today's money.

Eager to begin her studies after New Year's Day of 1935, Zora drove from Chicago to New York almost immediately upon learning that she had been awarded the grant. At the last moment, though, the Rosenwald Fund cut Zora's grant to seven hundred dollars—not enough for her to complete her doctorate degree. In order to at least receive the reduced amount, Zora attended classes occasionally at Columbia over the next few months, but she used most of the money to support herself while she wrote.

Although she now considered Florida her home, Zora made periodic trips to New York to attend a few classes at Columbia and to visit friends and promote her books. But she had another reason to spend time in the big city. During the mid-1930s the man to whom she referred as "the real love affair of my life" lived in New York. In her writings, Zora referred to him as P.M.P., but later research by her biographer Robert Hemenway revealed that his name was Percival McGuire Punter.

Percy, as she called him, had been born in New York City in 1912. The two had actually met back in 1931, when Percy had been one of the singers in Zora's production of *The Great Day*, her folk musical that had lasted just a single day at the John Golden Theatre. At that time, Zora had recently divorced Herbert Sheen and she wasn't interested in beginning a serious relationship with anyone. But more than three years later when Zora came to New York to begin collecting her Rosenwald Fund money, she and Percy met again and began dating.

In several ways, Zora and Percy were an unlikely pair. First, there was a huge age difference, for she was forty-four years old while he was only twenty-three. They came from vastly different backgrounds — Percy from the nation's biggest city and Zora from little Eatonville, Florida. Another difference was that Zora had established a career for herself. Percy, on the other hand, was thinking of studying for the ministry but wasn't at all sure about his future path in life. He worked at some kind of menial job while attending Columbia University in quest of his master's degree.

For a while these differences didn't interfere with their romance. "He was tall, dark brown, magnificently built," Zora wrote in her autobiography. "But his looks only drew my eyes. I did not fall in love with him just for that. He had a fine mind and that intrigued me. I did not just fall in love. I made a parachute jump."

After a few months, though, their love affair ran into snags. Percy didn't have much money, so sometimes he walked more than fifty blocks between

»»» "I love myself when I am laughing," Zora wrote. "And
then again when I am looking mean and impressive."

his and Zora's apartments to visit her. One night, Percy was ready to start the long walk home when Zora suddenly felt sorry for him and offered to lend him a quarter until his payday so that he could take public transportation. Percy was insulted. What did Zora think he was, a cream puff? He was a man and he didn't need charity to visit the woman he loved.

They had more serious disagreements. Percy was the jealous type and didn't like Zora even smiling at another man. In her apartment Zora had some photographs that her friend Carl Van Vechten had taken of her. While thanking Carl, whom she called "Pink-Toe" because of his light skin, Zora had written: "I love myself when I am laughing. And then again when I am looking mean and impressive." Percy pointed to a picture of Zora looking "mean and impressive" and said that he wanted her to look like that when she was with other people. The laughing and smiling Zora was to be only for him.

Their biggest clash was over her career. Percy was jealous that Zora hobnobbed with celebrities and always seemed to be going to teas and luncheons with Annie Nathan Meyer, Fannie Hurst, Bertram Lippincott, and Carl Van Vechten. Sometimes Percy accompanied her to these events, but he would just sit in a corner and sulk because he felt left out. After a while he refused to go with Zora to her literary get-togethers. In fact, he insisted that if Zora wanted to continue their relationship, she must give up her career and marry him.

Giving up writing for any man was impossible for Zora. "That one thing I could not do," she explained in her autobiography. "I had things clawing inside of me that must be said." Despite her deep love for Percy, she refused to surrender to his demand. Instead, she gave up "the real love affair" of her life in the spring of 1935. Later, Zora's lingering feelings for Percy would inspire her most famous book.

That June, right after she and Percy parted, Zora was hired to help two folklorists collect African American folk music in the South. One was Professor Mary Elizabeth Barnicle of New York University. The other was Alan Lomax, the twenty-year-old son and assistant to John Lomax, a prominent folklorist at the Library of Congress in Washington, D.C.

Zora led Professor Barnicle and young Lomax to African American communities in Georgia and Florida, where they made recordings of numerous folksingers. In her hometown of Eatonville, Zora arranged for an acquaintance of hers to play the guitar for Lomax and Barnicle. After hearing him play, Alan Lomax wrote: "Miss Hurston introduced us to the finest Negro guitarist I have ever heard, better even than Leadbelly." He was referring to Huddie "Leadbelly" Ledbetter, whom John and Alan Lomax had discovered in 1934 when he was an inmate of a Louisiana prison. Paroled into the Lomaxes' custody because of his talent as a folksinger, guitarist, and composer, Leadbelly by 1935 was on his way to becoming a performing and recording star. For Alan Lomax to rate the Eatonville musician "better even than Leadbelly" was enormous praise, but the man, whose name was Gabriel Brown, never gained fame comparable to Leadbelly's.

Unfortunately, Zora and Professor Barnicle did not get along. The last straw for Zora occurred when Barnicle insisted on photographing a young Eatonville boy eating a watermelon. For many years white people had portrayed black people happily eating watermelon in drawings, stories, and movies, and Zora was upset that Barnicle was perpetuating the stereotype. The two women argued over the picture. Zora became so angry that she quit as the guide for Lomax and Barnicle's folk-song collecting expedition.

Although Zora had the satisfaction of knowing that she had done the right thing, during the Great Depression jobs were scarce. After weeks of unsuccessful job hunting, Zora finally found work with a new government program designed to help unemployed Americans. She was hired as a drama coach for the Harlem Unit of the Federal Theatre Project. During her six months on the job, she helped coach actors and actresses in a production called *Walk Together Chillun*. Although she didn't think much of the show, she needed the $23.66 weekly paycheck, especially because her niece, Zora Mack, was living with her at about this time. Ten-year-old Zora was the daughter of Zora Neale Hurston's sister, Sarah, who had died at the age of only forty-four. Zora Mack later recalled that the aunt for whom she had been named took great care of her and bought her "gorgeous clothes" and other "beautiful things" during the few months they lived together.

In March 1936, Zora received wonderful news about a grant for which she had applied. The Guggenheim Foundation had awarded her two thousand dollars to study voodoo and other religious practices as well as the folklore of black people in the West Indies. Zora quit her job with the Federal Theatre Project and in April she departed by steamship for the islands in the Caribbean. Although she also traveled through Jamaica, Zora spent most of the next year and a half in Haiti, where voodoo had first taken root in the New World and where it was still practiced.

Among other things, Zora investigated zombies in Haiti. Zombies were said to be dead people who had been brought back to life by magical voodoo spells. Known as "the living dead," they were allegedly soulless beings with no minds of their own. As part of her research, Zora was invited by a Haitian doctor to meet an actual zombie in a government hospital. The story of this woman — Felicia Felix-Mentor — was extremely strange.

Felicia had supposedly died in 1907. Yet in 1936 she was found wandering about the countryside, muttering to herself, "This is the farm of my father. I used to live here." Her brother, the current owner of the farm, was astonished to see Felicia, for whom a death certificate had been issued twenty-nine years earlier. Zora snapped Felicia's picture — capturing the first known image of a zombie. She also wondered: How could a woman who had been pronounced dead in 1907 suddenly appear among the living, with, as Zora described it, a "blank face with dead eyes"? Was there something supernatural about it, or was there another explanation?

Zora did more investigating until she discovered the truth. Living people were made into zombies by being forced to take certain drugs. First they were given drugs to make them appear to be dead. Then they were given other drugs to revive them. In the drugging process portions of their brains were destroyed, frequently depriving them of the power of speech and the ability to make decisions. Far from being the frightening supernatural creatures portrayed in movies and horror stories, zombies such as Felicia Felix-Mentor were forced to work as slaves on plantations and farms.

While in Haiti, Zora began writing a book about zombies, voodoo, and the folklore of Haiti and Jamaica. She called it *Tell My Horse*. In a remarkable burst of creativity, in less than two months she also wrote her most famous book from beginning to end. Zora explained in her autobiography: "I wrote

»»» After her return from Haiti and Jamaica, Zora enjoyed demonstrating
voodoo drumming for her friends.

Their Eyes Were Watching God in Haiti. It was dammed up in me, and I wrote it in seven weeks."

Their Eyes, as it is known for short, is the story of a Florida girl, and then woman, named Janie Crawford and her lifelong quest for love and respect. After two failed marriages, Janie eventually finds what she is seeking in a younger man known as Tea Cake. From the first page to the last, *Their Eyes* is rich with realistic dialogue, poetic descriptions of Janie's feelings, and stunning depictions of nature. One of the book's most compelling passages describes Janie and Tea Cake's flight from a hurricane:

> They saw other people like themselves struggling along. A house down, here and there, frightened cattle. But above all the drive of the wind and the water. And the lake. Under its multiplied roar could be heard a mighty sound of grinding rock and timber and a wail. They looked back. Saw people trying to run in raging waters and screaming when they found they couldn't. The monstropolous beast had left his bed. The two hundred miles an hour wind had loosed his chains. The sea was walking the earth with a heavy heel.
>
> "De lake is comin'!" Tea Cake gasped.
>
> "It's comin' behind us!" Janie shuddered. "Us can't fly."

In her autobiography Zora explained that her lingering love for Percy Punter helped make *Their Eyes* a special book. "I tried," she wrote, "[to embody] all the tenderness of my passion for him in *Their Eyes Were Watching God*."

The novel would eventually become a bestseller, but unfortunately for Zora, that wouldn't happen for about half a century.

"I Shall Keep Trying"

ZORA RETURNED TO THE STATES in late September 1937. Her timing was superb. She had mailed the manuscript of *Their Eyes Were Watching God* from Haiti. Her editors had seen need for only a small number of changes, and Lippincott had published the book just a few days before her arrival in New York. Still "scared to *death* of reviews," Zora combed newspapers and magazines to see what the critics thought of her second novel.

Their Eyes received mostly outstanding reviews. The *New York Times* called it "a perfect story…simple and beautiful and shining with humor." Other reviewers agreed. Although the praise was gratifying, Zora was stung by a few negative reviews that came from her fellow black writers.

For one thing, they criticized Zora for writing a love story at a time when black Americans were suffering from discrimination. Wouldn't it be a better use of her talent for Zora to write a novel about how her people were mistreated? Furthermore, why did she have her characters say things like

"Us can't fly"? Such dialogue made it appear that black people couldn't speak proper English.

Zora was wounded by the criticism. She had grown up in Florida and had modeled her dialogue after the way people she knew really spoke. And who ordained that black authors should write only protest novels? What was wrong with a love story with black characters?

The criticism that hurt Zora the most came from her old professor, Alain Locke, who commented in *Opportunity* magazine that she would be better off writing about social issues. As she had done in her quarrel with Langston Hughes, Zora quickly went from feeling insulted to feeling enraged. She wrote a criticism of Locke's criticism, which she sent to *Opportunity*. Ripping into Locke like a lioness protecting her cub, Zora called Locke's review "an example of rank dishonesty" and "a fraud." "[He] knows nothing about Negroes," she continued, and "has not produced one single idea or suggestion of an idea that he can call his own." In fact, Zora added, Locke was so ignorant about their people that she offered to "send [her] toe-nails to debate him on what he knows about Negroes and Negro life."

Fortunately, *Opportunity* chose not to print Zora's hateful essay about Locke. Otherwise her friendship with the man who had helped her along in her career probably would have been shattered, as had happened with Langston Hughes seven years earlier. Zora also badmouthed Locke to their mutual friends. She wrote to James Weldon Johnson, "Alain Leroy Locke is a malicious, spiteful little snot that thinks he ought to be the leading Negro because of his degrees."

After promoting *Their Eyes Were Watching God* for a few weeks, Zora returned to Florida, where she worked on *Tell My Horse*, her folklore book about Haiti and Jamaica. Published in October 1938, *Tell My Horse* was criticized for lacking organization. This time Zora admitted that the criticism was deserved.

Their Eyes and *Tell My Horse* had one thing in common. During Zora's lifetime each book sold only a few thousand copies. Although she wasn't happy about the lack of sales, Zora didn't dwell on it. By the time *Tell My Horse* came out she had begun her next project: a novel called *Moses, Man of the Mountain* about the biblical hero.

Zora's Guggenheim Foundation grant had expired, so once again she needed to find a job while she wrote. In April 1938 she was hired by the Federal Writers' Project (FWP), a government program that employed needy writers. During her year and a half with the FWP, she was assigned to collect and edit material for *The Florida Negro*, a book that was intended to chronicle black life in her home state. Although she was paid only sixty-three dollars a month — less than what white FWP writers with virtually no experience earned — the job was perfect for Zora in several ways.

For one thing, she was able to base herself in Eatonville, making only periodic visits to Florida FWP headquarters in Jacksonville. For another, she was able to use folklore she had already collected over the years for *The Florida Negro*. The job also allowed her what she craved: lots of time to herself. She needed to work on her new novel about Moses, and to care for her nieces Wilhelmina and Winifred Hurston, who lived with her for several months during this period. The girls had come to stay with Aunt Zora following the death of their father, Dr. Bob Hurston, in Memphis, Tennessee.

While living with her aunt Zora, twenty-year-old Wilhelmina fell in love with a local orange grove worker and married him. Winifred, who was two years younger than Wilhelmina, later recalled what life with her aunt was like. Zora, she explained, liked to do things on the spur of the moment. She once asked Winifred to accompany her on a trip to Jacksonville. Assuming that her aunt intended to go in a few days, Winifred accepted the invitation. "Let's go!" Zora said, and the two of them jumped into the car and drove off to Jacksonville, 135 miles away, then and there. Winifred also told relatives that she didn't think her aunt was the marrying kind: "Aunt Zora doesn't have any business with a husband. She doesn't have time for that. 'Cause she likes to go when she gets ready. She [doesn't] want anyone to tell her 'don't go, don't do,' or something like that."

But on one of her trips to Jacksonville, Zora met Albert Price III, a twenty-three-year-old college student who at the time was employed by a government program as a playground worker. Zora and Albert were married outside Jacksonville on June 27, 1939. On their marriage license, Zora set her personal record for lying about her age. Although she was actually forty-eight years old, she claimed that she was born in 1910 and was only twenty-nine!

Zora should have listened to her niece Winifred. As with her marriage to Herbert Sheen, her marriage to Albert Price III was a failure. Zora soon left her young husband. Among her complaints was her claim that Albert used foul language and threatened to beat her up. She also objected to his expectation that she live with him at his mother's house. Living with a mother-in-law who may have actually been younger than she was did not appeal to Zora.

Albert had his own complaints: He said that Zora had a ferocious temper and threatened to harm him with the "voodooism" that she had learned in Haiti. Her friends thought that Zora had married Albert only because he reminded her of her true love, Percy Punter. In any event, the couple separated after just six weeks and later divorced.

The *Florida Negro* project was another disappointment to Zora. The two-hundred-page book was to feature black Floridians' music, folklore, and expressions, as well as narratives of former slaves. The following is one of the "lies" Zora planned to include:

> *They have strong winds on the Florida west coast. One day the wind blowed so hard till it blowed a well out of the ground. Then one day it blowed so hard till it blowed a crooked road straight. Another time it blowed and blowed and scattered the days of the week so bad till Sunday didn't come until late Tuesday evening.*

For reasons that are not clear, the book was not published.

Around the time that she left Albert Price III, Zora also quit her job with the Federal Writers' Project. She wasn't unemployed for long. By October, Zora had been hired to head the Drama Department of North Carolina College for Negroes in Durham. At first the school's president and founder, Dr. James E. Shepard, was pleased to have the widely published author teaching drama to his students. Zora was happy with the job, especially since it gave her time to write.

Zora had been teaching at the college only a few weeks when Lippincott published *Moses, Man of the Mountain*. One of the most unusual pieces of writing of Zora's career, the novel featured a Moses who was a black man. Like *Their Eyes Were Watching God*, her new novel was ripped into by Alain Locke and a few other black authors, who insisted that Zora should write about contemporary problems.

Although Zora disagreed with Locke, she did feel that she could have done a better job writing the novel. "I don't think it achieved all that I set out to do," she admitted to a friend. "I thought that in this book I would achieve my ideal, but it seems that I have not reached it yet but I shall keep trying." Zora took comfort in the thought that her career was a work in progress and that her best books lay in the future.

Within a few months, Zora was at odds with the college president. Shepard expected his female faculty members to live on campus, but Zora insisted on living in a log cabin in the woods, where she had nothing to distract her from her writing. She accused the college of failing to offer its students classes in playwriting and theater production while expecting her to somehow have the students present plays. In March 1940, after about half a year at the college, Zora resigned.

For the next few years, she worked at one job after another, none of them lasting for more than a year. The anthropologist Jane Belo hired Zora to assist her in a study of African American churches in South Carolina. Zora went out to California, where she was hired by the Hollywood movie studio Paramount to work as a writer. Paramount paid her $100 a week — equivalent to $1,500 today and the highest salary Zora would ever earn. However, Zora objected to the way black actors mostly played servants, cooks, and wisecracking clowns in Hollywood movies. Besides, she wasn't able to persuade the studio to film any of her books. Despite the hefty salary, Zora resigned from Paramount after only two months.

She went on the lecture circuit—speaking at black colleges about her books. She taught literature at Florida Normal and Industrial College in St. Augustine. That job didn't last either, because, as usual, Zora didn't get along with the school's officials. During World War II, Zora served in Florida's Recreation in War program, which was created to entertain soldiers who were stationed at bases throughout the state. She probably read to the troops from her books and amused them by singing folk songs while playing her guitar. For a time Zora also was a paid political worker for a congressional candidate in Harlem.

Zora had moved around so often that she changed addresses dozens of times over the course of her life. In 1943 she found a way to take her home with her as she traveled. She bought a houseboat, which she named the *Wanago*. Zora lived on that vessel and on a later boat called the *Sun Tan* for four years during the 1940s. She became a skilled captain, taking her floating home up and down Florida waterways. On one occasion she piloted the *Wanago* all the way from Florida to New York City—a voyage of some 1,500 miles. Zora loved to fish from her houseboats and, as she told author Marjorie Kinnan Rawlings, the vessels provided her with "that solitude that I love."

Yet Zora also suffered from loneliness during the 1940s. She didn't have many close friends in Florida, and neither did she have as many friends to visit on her periodic trips to New York as she once had. The Harlem Renaissance had ended by the late 1930s, and many of her old friends had departed from the scene. Wallace Thurman of the short-lived *Fire!!* magazine had died in 1934. Four years later James Weldon Johnson died in an automobile-train collision — much like Zora's own father. "Papa Franz" Boas, her anthropology professor at Columbia, died in 1942, and the poet Countee Cullen's death occurred in 1946. Ill and unable to write letters or receive many visitors, "Godmother" Charlotte Mason spent her last thirteen years at New York Hospital, where she died in 1946 at the age of ninety-one. And of course Zora was no longer close to several New York friends, including Langston Hughes and Alain Locke, whom she had once fondly called "Old Cabbage."

Loneliness was undoubtedly a big reason why Zora decided to try marriage one more time. On January 18, 1944 — just two months after her divorce from Albert Price III was finalized — Zora married again. Her new husband was James Howell Pitts, a forty-five-year-old businessman from Cleveland, Ohio. Although Zora had celebrated her fifty-third birthday three days before the wedding, she claimed on the marriage license to be only forty years old. Zora and James were married in the vicinity of Daytona Beach, Florida, where she docked the *Wanago*.

James and Zora did not get along after being married. He may have objected to living on a houseboat. Certainly Zora wasn't about to give up her floating home just because her new husband preferred to live on land. In any case, Winifred's pronouncement "Aunt Zora doesn't have any business with a husband" soon proved true once again. Zora and James were divorced on Halloween 1944, just nine months after they had exchanged their wedding vows.

Zora's third marriage was so brief that many people who knew her never realized that she and James Howell Pitts had ever been husband and wife.

Between 1940 and 1948, while Zora went from job to job and divorced two husbands, there was one constant in her life: her writing. She was producing as much or more than she had in her younger years. She wrote book reviews for magazines and newspapers. She was hired to write encyclopedia entries relating to African Americans. She sold articles to the *Saturday Evening Post* and other major magazines. Zora also worked on book proposals and manuscripts that she sent to Lippincott. After publishing *Moses, Man of the Mountain* in 1939, however, the firm turned down several of Zora's proposals and partially written books.

In the early 1940s Bertram Lippincott made a suggestion to Zora. Why not write her life story? Zora objected, saying that she was still in her prime and that autobiographies were for authors who were old and unable to write regular books anymore. But, failing to interest Bertram Lippincott in any of her other ideas, Zora reluctantly agreed to write her autobiography. "I did not want to do it now, but my publisher wanted it very much," Zora told a friend. She wrote her autobiography, *Dust Tracks on a Road*, over the period of about a year and a half in 1941–1942.

Zora had a big problem with recounting her life story. How could she create her autobiography without revealing that she was much older than she claimed? In the end she did it by providing few dates and by skipping over certain periods of her life. She also lied about some key facts. For example, Zora claimed to have been born in Eatonville, Florida, when she knew very well that her birthplace was Notasulga, Alabama. She also omitted episodes in her

He's a dark brown, stockily built Negro of the cow lands of Central Florida—and his story is a symbol of the strength of our nation.

RALPH PIERSON

Lawrence of the River

By ZORA NEALE HURSTON
A Distinguished Negro Novelist

THIS is about a man of the cow lands of Florida. The heart of cow Florida is the Kissimmee Prairie, which stretches for more than a hundred miles from just south of Orlando to the upper Everglades. It embraces the headwaters of the St. Johns River and it gives Florida high rank among the beef producers of the Union.

Lawrence Silas, a dark brown, stockily built Negro, is in and of the cow lands. He is important, because his story is a sign and a symbol of the strength of the nation. It helps to explain our history, and makes a promise for the future. Lawrence Silas represents the men who could plan and do, the generations who were willing to undertake the hard job—to accept the challenge of the frontiers. And remember, he had one more frontier to conquer than the majority of men in America. He speaks for free enterprise and personal initiative. That is America.

Considering that Florida is in Dixie, it will sound like poker playing at a prayer meeting when you read that Lawrence Silas, Negro, is one of the important men of the cow country. But that is the word with the bark on it. The cattlemen of the state have a name for him, and it is good.

They talk about him readily, and with admiration. They do not tell you about his thousands of head of cattle, his fifty-odd miles of fence, or his chunky bank account. They like more to tell you about his character and his skill, as if to say that you ought to have sense enough to know that a man like that is just bound to have something to put away.

When I called Silas' attention to this recently, he replied quietly: "Well, I have never had my word doubted in business. My plan is: Treat everybody right and honest; pay your just and honest debts; and tell the truth. Whenever you find a man that ain't right, why, feed him with a long-handled spoon. Pass and repass when you find out he won't deal right."

"But," I said, "you handle a lot of horses. How about horse trading? Don't you have to lie in a horse deal?"

"Some folks do a powerful lot of it, so they must figure they have to. I don't see it that way. If I think somebody is interested in buying, I tell 'em I want to sell the horse. I give so much for him, and I got to have so much for him. He ain't no good to me, but maybe he is all right for you. In that way, nobody can't say I lied to beat him out of his money. Then we don't lose no friendship over the deal."

"As simple as that?"

"Sure. In the first place, I know horses too well to let anybody sell me any crow bait, and then the people know that I know what I'm doing, so any horse I ever own would be good for somebody. They might not suit for what *I* want."

Silas knows horses, their uses and treatment, from nose to fetlock, and cows from horns to tail brush. The other breeders know that he knows. Therefore, the richest dealers and breeders in the business will come to him for expert advice before buying or selling herds.

He buys and sells for Lykes Brothers, one of the biggest outfits in the world. Young Pat Johnson, whose father was one of the Florida pioneers in the game, comes to him for advice as he would to a father. If Lawrence Silas says it is so, then it is so. So be it in the grand lodge.

By repute, his hands are as skilled as his mind and eyes. He can sit on a gap, which is what the cow people call a corral gate, and let the cowboys run—actually run—a herd of cattle past him. No matter how large the herd, amount of dust or the speed, when the last steer has passed he can tell you exactly how many passed the gap. He never misses one—or adds one. *(Continued on Page 55)*

»»» Zora published her first *Saturday Evening Post* article about a black Florida landowner in September 1942.

life that had turned out unpleasantly, such as her friendship and dispute with Langston Hughes.

When it came out in November 1942, *Dust Tracks* received mostly good reviews. It even won the Anisfield-Wolf Award as "the best book of the year concerned with racial problems in the field of creative literature," which came with a prize of a thousand dollars. But in later years, biographers researching her life discovered Zora's misleading information and falsehoods, prompting an onslaught of criticism, especially from other black authors. For instance, Alice Walker, a great Hurston fan, blasted *Dust Tracks* as "the most unfortunate thing Zora ever wrote," adding, "After the first several chapters, it rings false." Others have sarcastically referred to *Dust Tracks* as one of Zora Neale Hurston's best works of fiction.

Yet most people agree that the first few chapters of *Dust Tracks* — relating to Zora's childhood and youth — are beautifully written and basically accurate. And some people, such as the author Valerie Boyd, passionately argue that while portions of the book may be unreliable regarding dates and places, *Dust Tracks* does an outstanding job of describing Zora's feelings at various stages of her life. Like everything else about Zora Neale Hurston, her autobiography remains controversial and stirs up strong feelings in its readers to this day.

What Zora really wanted was to sell another novel to Lippincott, but in this she failed repeatedly. By September 1945 she had written two-thirds of a novel titled *Mrs. Doctor*, about wealthy African Americans. Lippincott turned it down. Next she began a novel set in Eatonville about a young man who is kicked out of town and experiences a series of adventures before returning seven years later. Lippincott rejected this would-be novel also.

»»» Alice Walker, author of *The Color Purple*, spearheaded the revival of Zora Neale Hurston's
books. In this photo Ms. Walker is signing books at one of Eatonville's annual
Zora Neale Hurston Festivals of the Arts and Humanities.

Amid all these rejections, Zora became involved in what today seems like a crackpot scheme. In the mid-1940s an Englishman named Reginald Brett and his wife visited Zora. For several years, Brett had been in the Central American country of Honduras, mining gold. He had read *Tell My Horse*, Brett informed Zora, and so he knew that she was a noted folklorist. There was a treasury of folklore among the people of Honduras, Brett explained. Furthermore, he said that he had been the first non-Indian to see the ruins of an ancient Mayan city in Honduras. The lost city would be a wonderful topic for Zora to write about, and it might even contain buried treasure, Brett claimed.

One thing that comes to mind is that Brett was a con man who planned to swindle Zora. But this seems unlikely, because Zora didn't have much of anything to be swindled out of. Perhaps Brett really had glimpsed some Mayan ruins and believed he had seen a lost city. Anyway, Zora fully believed him. She was so excited by his story that for about three years she tried in vain to raise money for an expedition to Honduras.

While trying to finance the lost city expedition, Zora also worked on *Seraph on the Suwanee*. This new novel was about another Florida woman searching for love, only this time the character was white.

It was beginning to dawn on Zora that Lippincott was no longer eager to publish her works, perhaps because they didn't sell very well. Since the early 1940s Zora had been friendly on and off with her fellow Florida author Marjorie Kinnan Rawlings, whose novel *The Yearling* had won the 1939 Pulitzer Prize. On one occasion Miss Rawlings spent a week with Zora aboard the *Wanago*. Miss Rawlings had an outstanding publisher, Scribner, where she worked with the nation's most prominent book editor, Maxwell Perkins.

Known for his ability to prod authors to write and rewrite a manuscript until it was the best it could be, Perkins had edited books by such famous writers as Ernest Hemingway and F. Scott Fitzgerald. In early 1947, Miss Rawlings spoke to Perkins and persuaded him to consider taking on Zora Neale Hurston as a new author.

That April, Zora met at least twice with Maxwell Perkins in his New York office. The editor was excited by Zora's description of *Seraph on the Suwanee*, and he probably read at least a few pages of her novel-in-progress. He was so confident of the novel's potential that after the second interview he offered Zora a contract including a five-hundred-dollar advance.

After fourteen years of being published by Lippincott, Zora was thrilled to switch to Scribner and to work with an editor who had faith in her. At the age of fifty-six, she felt that her writing career was about to be reborn under Maxwell Perkins.

Almost immediately upon receiving her advance, Zora spent a chunk of it on a ticket to travel to Honduras by ocean liner. Her plan was to find a quiet spot to finish *Seraph on the Suwanee* and then search for the lost city that Reginald Brett had described. Zora sailed to Honduras in early May. After visiting the capital city of Tegucigalpa, she settled in a hotel in the town of Puerto Cortes along the Caribbean Sea.

Zora had been steadfastly working on her novel for a month when on June 21, 1947, she wrote a letter to her friend Carl Van Vechten saying, "I feel lucky to be under Max Perkins." She hadn't yet been informed that Perkins had died just four days earlier. His death was a blow to all the authors who worked with him, but especially to Zora, who was about to do her first book

»»» Scribner provided this publicity photo for Zora's
Seraph on the Suwanee, which they published in 1948.

with him. Soon Zora heard from her new editor at Scribner, Burroughs Mitchell, who sent her an additional five hundred dollars, which she had requested, along with a note saying, "I hope that tells you we have great confidence in this new book of yours."

Zora wound up spending about six months in her hotel room completing the first draft and then rewriting *Seraph on the Suwanee.* Around November 1 she sent the manuscript to New York. Zora then set out for the rainforests of what is called the Mosquito Coast of northeastern Honduras. She didn't find any lost city, and soon returned to Puerto Cortes, apparently because of the heavy rains. The rains continued — "18 inches here in three days" she informed Burroughs Mitchell—which prevented her from heading back to the Mosquito Coast to resume her search.

Zora was still waiting for the rain to stop when Burroughs Mitchell sent her a message requesting that she come to New York to work with him on revising *Seraph on the Suwanee*. Determined to one day return to Honduras to make a more thorough search for the lost city, Zora sailed for New York in February 1948. She had spent more than nine months in Honduras, writing her book, exploring, and waiting for the rain to stop.

Back in New York, Zora worked with Mitchell on the revisions for her novel, which was published in the fall. Perhaps with Maxwell Perkins editing it, *Seraph on the Suwanee* would have been a rousing success. As it was, the novel received some poor reviews, including one from the *New York Times* that called its characters "half-human puppets." Reviews like this limited the novel's sales to 4,600 copies.

By this time, though, Zora was working on new projects that she felt had more potential than any of her previous work. She still believed that a glorious future awaited her.

Zora couldn't have known it, but she would never publish another book in her lifetime, and returning to search for the lost city would remain only a dream.

12

"I Had Exactly Four Pennies"

WHEN *SERAPH ON THE SUWANEE* APPEARED in October 1948, it was Zora's seventh published book. It might be expected that with four novels, two books of folklore, and an autobiography to her credit, Zora would have a tidy sum of money in the bank. Instead she had no savings and very little income. She was even reduced to leaving her typewriter in a pawnshop in exchange for a little cash, and asking friends to help her out.

"Please help me," Zora wrote to Fannie Hurst on February 10, 1949, while in New York. "You know that I would not cry out for help unless I was really desperate. What I must have now is enough to keep me alive for two weeks. I owe room rent now and other things. I have used up every available resource before appealing to you—even to pawning my typewriter. I have counted up and find that I must get hold of 76.00 at once." Upon receiving Zora's plea, Fannie Hurst sent her a check, as did other old friends and acquaintances.

Things brightened up a little for Zora in June 1949 when she sold a short story to the *Saturday Evening Post.* "The Conscience of the Court" was about a black servant who proves her loyalty to the white woman for whom she works. The *Saturday Evening Post* paid Zora nine hundred dollars for the story — enough to help get her through the summer. By then she had begun a new novel, *The Lives of Barney Turk,* chronicling the adventures of a Florida farmboy who visits Honduras, joins the military, and eventually winds up in Hollywood.

In late 1949 Zora returned to Florida. With few exceptions, she would remain in her favorite state for the rest of her life, living at different times in Miami, Belle Glade, Eau Gallie, Merritt Island, and Fort Pierce. Early in 1950 the fifty-nine-year-old author was hired as a maid by the Burritt family in the Miami suburb of Rivo Alto Island. Although Zora told the newspaper reporter that she liked "to cook and keep house," evidently at her age she found the job exhausting. As a result, she was slow to make the revisions on *Barney Turk* that Burroughs Mitchell requested. After newspapers ran stories with such headlines as "SUCCESSFUL AUTHOR WORKING AS A MAID," Zora left that job. With the money she had saved working for the Burritts — and now with the time and the energy to work again on her book — she at long last revised *Barney Turk.*

Despite the revisions, in October 1950 Burroughs Mitchell rejected Zora's newest novel, saying that *Barney Turk* was below her usual level of writing. Perhaps the problem was that Zora wasn't as comfortable writing about white people as she was at describing those she knew best — African Americans. We will never know for sure, because the manuscript for *The Lives of Barney Turk* no longer exists.

THE CONSCIENCE OF THE COURT

By ZORA NEALE HURSTON

The judge was ashamed.
An unlettered witness reminded
him of something
he had learned years ago—
and almost forgotten.

»»» The 1950 publication of "The Conscience of the Court" by the *Saturday Evening Post* was, Zora said, "One slam of a publicity do-dad." However, it cost her the job as a maid that she really needed at the time.

Zora was especially upset by the rejection because she had spent an entire year writing and rewriting *Barney Turk*. She must have realized that she was best at writing about her own people, though, for she chose a famous African American as the subject for her next novel. Her name was Sarah Breedlove Walker. Born in Louisiana to ex-slaves, "Madame C. J. Walker," as she was known, founded a company that made hair products for black women. Her business was so successful that Mrs. Walker became the first female black millionaire. By January 1951 Zora was writing a novel called *The Golden Bench of God* based on Madame C. J. Walker's life.

She had to overcome severe hardships to complete the project. Right before she received a one-hundred-dollar check for an article she had written, her financial situation was grim: "I had exactly four pennies," Zora wrote to a friend on March 18, 1951. Six days later Zora was found nearly unconscious at the house where she was staying in Belle Glade, Florida. She was rushed to a hospital, where doctors said she was suffering from influenza with complications. She was hospitalized for fifteen days, and even after returning home she had trouble concentrating on her work.

Zora finally managed to complete *The Golden Bench of God* and send it to Burroughs Mitchell. With a fascinating subject such as Madame C. J. Walker, Zora expected *The Golden Bench* to be snapped up by Scribner and perhaps be made into a Hollywood movie. She was once again deeply disappointed when in July 1951 Mitchell rejected her manuscript, saying "We can't feel that this novel comes close to success." We will never know how good *The Golden Bench* was either, because like *Barney Turk*, it has disappeared.

Scribner's rejection of her novels meant that Zora still had to find other jobs at an age when many people were retiring. In fact, she had some of her most unusual jobs later in life. After leaving the Burritts', Zora worked in the campaign office of George Smathers, who ran for a U.S. Senate seat from Florida in 1950. During the campaign, George Smathers's father, the retired judge Frank Smathers, made Zora an offer. The judge wanted to write his autobiography. However, he was an elderly man for whom writing was difficult. Would Zora ghostwrite the story of his life for him?

Zora agreed to serve as the judge's ghostwriter—meaning that for a fee she would write his book while he received all the credit as the author. She spent long hours listening to the judge's life story, taking notes, and starting to write the book. The problem was, Judge Smathers was used to bossing everyone around. Zora wrote to her editor Burroughs Mitchell that the "old cuss" constantly bullied his wife as well as his son George, who was about to become a U.S. senator. When Judge Smathers tried to browbeat Zora into writing his autobiography exactly as he said it, she pointed out that she was his ghostwriter, not his secretary. There was another issue. As Zora informed her editor, "He could not accept the reality that a descendant of slaves could do something in an intellectual way that he could not."

Judge Smathers had a habit of sticking his fingers in his ears whenever anyone said something he disagreed with. When he pulled this stunt with Zora, she reached over and yanked his fingers out of his ears, then finished talking. "We fought like tigers, from day to day," Zora told her editor, "and I came to see that he loved it." But while the judge enjoyed matching wits with her, Zora disliked his bullying ways and the frequent battles. She quit as his ghostwriter before the book was completed. Frank Smathers's autobiography was eventually published in 1958, but how much of Zora's material made it into the final version is not known.

Zora also worked as a newspaper reporter in her later years. In August 1952 an African American woman named Ruby McCollum shot a white doctor to death in the town of Live Oak, Florida. Ruby McCollum was charged with murder, and when it was revealed that she had been the doctor's girl-friend, her trial drew a nationwide following. Zora was asked to cover the story for the *Pittsburgh Courier*, one of the nation's most popular black newspapers.

Zora went to Live Oak and sat through weeks of testimony at the trial. She also interviewed Ruby and her friends and relatives. The result was a ten-part series for the *Courier* titled "The Life Story of Mrs. Ruby J. McCollum!" Zora's series was one of the most sympathetic portraits written about Ruby McCol-lum, who was originally sentenced to die in the electric chair. Many people credit Zora with helping to overturn the death sentence for McCollum, who instead of being executed was placed in a mental institution. Some of Zora's writings on the case were included in the 1956 book *Ruby McCollum: Woman in the Suwannee Jail* by the journalist William Bradford Huie.

But Zora was still determined to sell a book of her own to a publisher. For many years she had wanted to write a book about Jewish history, possibly because a number of people who helped her early in her career were Jewish, including Annie Nathan Meyer, Fannie Hurst, and Franz Boas. Back in 1945 Zora had written to Carl Van Vechten, "The story I am burning to write is ... the story of the 3000 years struggle of the Jewish people for democracy and the rights of man." Zora spent most of the 1950s researching, writing, and rewriting a manuscript about ancient Jewish history. She worked at this project, *Herod the Great*, longer and more intensely than she had for any other book in her life. In October 1953 she wrote to Burroughs Mitchell that she was "under the spell of a great obsession. The life story of HEROD THE GREAT. You have no idea the great amount of research that I have done on this man."

Creating *Herod the Great* may have been the most heroic accomplishment of Zora's life. During the writing of this book she suffered at various times from intestinal trouble, ulcers, a gall bladder infection, a tropical virus she had picked up from drinking polluted water in Honduras, and high blood pressure. Now that she was more than sixty years old and afflicted by all these conditions, she had far less energy than she had formerly possessed. Yet, writing steadily, she completed half the manuscript by the middle of 1954 and nearly the whole book by June 1955. With her usual high hopes, a short time later Zora sent *Herod the Great* to Burroughs Mitchell at Scribner.

The verdict arrived in Zora's mail in late July. Mitchell reported that he was "truly sorry" to say that he had found *Herod the Great* "difficult" to read and disappointing. Scribner turned down Zora's manuscript.

Considering that she had spent a decade planning and writing this book, Zora was remarkably calm about the rejection. "Naturally, I am sorry that you found HEROD THE GREAT disappointing, but do not feel concerned about the refusal upon me," she wrote to Burroughs Mitchell. "I am my old self and can take it easily."

Zora handled the rejection well because she felt confident that she would sell *Herod the Great* elsewhere. She spent the rest of her life revising the manuscript. Periodically she sent her new versions to a few publishers, but they

FLORIDA PERSONALITY

Zora Hurston Sees King Herod Play As Her "GREATEST WORK"

By LEO SCHUMAKER

EAU GALLIE

In this coastal town that nestles down beside the languid waters of the Indian River one of the country's foremost novelists and folklore authorities has settled down to, as she puts it, "turn out her greatest work."

According to Zora Neale Hurston, this will be a play based on the life of King Herod, on whom she has a crush similar to a teenager for Tony Curtis.

"Old Herod led such a fabulous career he puts all the rest of them in the shade," Miss Hurston chuckled the other day, going on to relate some of the ancient Biblical character's exploits.

To the reader of her many books and short stories, the meeting of Miss Hurston is according to Hoyle. She is as full of exuberance and zest for living as many of the colorful persons she writes about.

Florida Native

Zora Hurston was born on January 7, 1903 in Eatonville, near Orlando. She attended high school at Morgan Academy of Morgan College at Baltimore and started college at Howard University. She later transferred to Barnard College in her sophomore year and took her B. A. there in 1928.

Dr. Franz Boaz obtained for her a fellowship in anthropology at Columbia University to do research in folklore, and immediately upon graduation she returned to her native South. By reason of four years' work in this field, Miss Hurston was invited to join the American Folklore Society, American Ethnological Society and American Anthropological Society. While working in the field—she was awarded the Mrs. R. Osgood Mason fellowship to study in the south and the Bahamas two years and a Guggenheim Fellowship for study in Haiti and the British West Indies for two years — she began to think of writing and decided to write about her people as they are, and not use the traditional lay figures.

First Book in 1934

Her first book, Jonah's Gourd Vine, was published in 1934 and met with instant critical acclaim. Her other books include Mules and Men, Their Eyes Were Watching God, Tell My Horse, Moses, Men of the Mountain, Seraph on the Suwanee, and Dust Tracks on a Road, her autobiography.

Miss Hurston's short stories and articles have appeared in Forum, Saturday Review, American Mercury and Saturday Evening Post, and many have appeared in various anthologies.

A life-long foe of Communism, although she was ardently courted by left-wingers because of her wide literary reputation, Miss Hurston created a sensation with her Post articles, Why the Negro Did Not Buy Communism and A Negro Voter Sizes Up Taft.

She is author of From Sun to Sun, a folklore concert drama, and had five sketches in the Broadway musical comedy production, Fast and Furious.

Miss Hurston says she is back at work in earnest now after a layoff to treat an ulcer.

"You wouldn't think I'd ever have an ulcer, would you? she laughed.

No, and then again, yes. For behind that infectious laughter is a brilliant mind keenly alert to the fast moving events of today's world.

»»» Zora spent the 1950s in Florida working on *Herod the Great.*

»»» During the 1950s, Zora continued writing, although her health was failing.

rejected it as Scribner had. From the portions of the manuscript that survive, it is apparent that *Herod the Great* is not nearly up to the quality of Zora's earlier books and that as she aged her writing ability declined along with her health.

It was even harder on Zora to know that by the mid-1950s all of her books were out of print. With her publishers no longer printing her books, Zora had less income than ever. Despite her failing health, she was forced to work almost until the end of her life.

In June 1956, sixty-five-year-old Zora was hired to work as a librarian at Patrick Air Force Base near Cocoa Beach, Florida. By Zora's standards she kept this job a long time: about a year. However, in 1957 her supervisor fired her, saying she was "too well educated for the job."

Zora's last job may have been the most difficult of all. In February 1958 she was asked to teach English at Lincoln Park Academy, a high school for African American students in Fort Pierce, Florida, where Zora had settled. The sixty-seven-year-old author was assigned to what was considered the worst-behaved homeroom in the school. Zora later reported, "Discipline at Lincoln Park Academy is terrible," and that the students had "the habit of toting knives" to school. Zora improved her pupils' behavior and the students liked and respected her. The job lasted only a short while, though, apparently because she lacked a Florida teaching certificate.

Zora rented her small house in Fort Pierce from a doctor named C. C. Benton. Seeing that she was having trouble taking care of herself, Dr. Benton visited Zora frequently. He treated her ailments and invited her over to his home for dinner every Sunday. It was said that toward the end of Zora's life

»»» This 1950s photo of Zora and her Florida friends was among the signed papers rescued by Patrick Duval.

neighborhood children also visited her almost daily, and that she would tell them folktales.

By 1959, though, there were more and more days when Zora was bed-ridden. She could no longer afford her prescription medicines and groceries, so that spring she went on welfare. In October she suffered a stroke. Because she had no money, Zora was soon admitted to the St. Lucie County Welfare Home, a nursing home in Fort Pierce for impoverished black people. She lived at the welfare home for three months. On January 28, 1960, Zora had another stroke. She died the same day at about seven o'clock in the evening. She had turned sixty-nine years old just thirteen days earlier.

At the time of her death Zora hadn't published a book in twelve years and was nearly forgotten as a writer. She didn't leave enough money for her funeral expenses, so people who had known her donated funds to provide her with a proper burial. Her publishers, Lippincott and Scribner, each gave one hundred dollars. Relatives and friends also sent money. But Zora probably would have appreciated one small contribution the most.

Her former Lincoln Park Academy students pooled their pennies and nickels and made a $2.50 donation for Miss Hurston, the elderly woman who had briefly been their teacher.

»»» Painter and printmaker Prentiss Taylor (AKA Baxter Snark) took this 1935 picture of Zora in New York City.

"Nothing Is Destructible": The Rebirth of Zora Neale Hurston

IN HER AUTOBIOGRAPHY, Zora wrote that she didn't fear death:

Nothing is destructible; things merely change forms. When the consciousness we know as life ceases, I know that I shall still be part and parcel of the world. I was a part before the sun rolled into shape. I was, when the earth was hurled out from its fiery rim. I shall return with the earth to Father Sun, and still exist in substance when the sun has lost its fire, and disintegrated in infinity to perhaps become a part of the whirling rubble in space. Why fear? The stuff of my being is matter, ever changing, ever moving, but never lost.

For many years, though, it appeared that her books and her reputation as an author were very "destructible." At the time of her death, all of Zora's books were out of print. They were at some libraries, but generally her published works were difficult to find. To make matters worse, a number of her original manuscripts were destroyed because of a terrible mistake.

One evening shortly after Zora died, Deputy Sheriff Patrick Duval was driving past her house in Fort Pierce when he noticed a column of smoke in the backyard. Stopping to investigate, Duval discovered that several people who had been hired to clean out the house were burning a trunkful of Zora's papers. Unaware that she had once been a prominent author, they had assumed that the papers were just old junk. Duval, however, knew that Zora was a writer and so he grabbed a garden hose, doused the flames, and gathered what was left of her papers.

Several original manuscripts, evidently including *The Lives of Barney Turk*, *The Golden Bench of God*, and much of *Herod the Great*, were destroyed, but Duval had saved some of Zora Neale Hurston's other manuscripts. He stored the papers on his porch for more than a year before finding someone who was interested in taking them. The papers, including some that were partially burned, were placed in the collections of the Department of Rare Books and Manuscripts at the University of Florida in Gainesville.

By the early 1970s, Zora's books—especially *Their Eyes Were Watching God*—were being rediscovered by a new generation of black women authors and teachers. As they read Zora's works, they fell in love with Janie Crawford, Tea Cake, and Zora's other characters. They were astonished by how real Zora's dialogue sounded. They also admired Zora's life story as an author:

5.

would be a mighty fine thing, the harried older women thought, if more girls felt as Arvay did. Therefore, on that day of Arvay's re-nunciation, when the girl had finished off by ~~tearfully~~ asking the prayers of the congregation, ~~for~~ their earnest prayers that she might hold out and never, never turn back, but ~~to~~ go on and on to greater grace, "Amens" burst out all over the church. The pastor himself had gotten to his feet and paid his young sister-in-law a great tribute.

" This young girl's devotion to the cause of Christ makes me feel ashamed," Reverend Middleton had (stated with an apostolic look on his face) " Here she is, much too young to be sent into the field as yet, but ready and willing to go. Ready to go wherever the Spirit might send her. Her stand ought to make me, and all of us grown folks feel ashamed. And if you, my flock ~~xxxx~~ feel that you can spare me, I will declare myself ready and willing to go."

The flock had cried some more at the thought of the pastor's offer to sacrifice himself, but it was felt that he could not be spared. To compenstae for this denial, the parsonage was re-painted, and five dollars a month was added to his salary, bringing the total to seventy dollars a month even.

Five years had passed since Arvay had turned her back on the world and all it's sins and snares. Arvay still played the entine the Sunday School, and she took an active part in chur the dose she kept strictly to herself. It was not too difficult the the community soon put Arvay Henson down a que blow " tetched." Nothing like her sister Rai on the ~~ever been~~ robust, not to say a trifle was pretty in the ways that the ru on har full head of curly reddish hair was li and full of ch

Gal. 3

»»» Also burned in the fire at Zora's house was this manuscript page from her 1948 novel *Seraph on the Suwanee.*

her refusal to give up despite numerous rejections, her writing book after book despite poverty and illness, her toughness in defending her work against unjust criticism, and her cheerful confidence that her next book would be her best.

The trouble was, for years after her death Zora's books remained hard to find. The new generation of Zora fans combed libraries and secondhand bookshops, searching for her books. When they found copies, they shared them. Sometimes they made photocopies of *Their Eyes Were Watching God* and other works by Zora for their friends and students.

Then in 1975, *Ms.* magazine published an article about Zora by Alice Walker, an African American author who later won the Pulitzer Prize for her novel *The Color Purple*. Titled "In Search of Zora Neale Hurston," Walker's article described her visit to Fort Pierce, Florida, to place a headstone on Zora's grave. Zora got the last laugh about her age, for, like just about everyone else, Alice Walker believed that Zora had been born much later than was actually the case. The headstone reads:

ZORA NEALE HURSTON
"A GENIUS OF THE SOUTH"
1901–1960
NOVELIST, FOLKLORIST
ANTHROPOLOGIST

Two years after the *Ms.* article, in 1977, Robert Hemenway published a book about Zora's life, *Zora Neale Hurston: A Literary Biography*. Alice Walker's article and Robert Hemenway's book helped spark a huge Zora revival.

In recent decades all of Zora's previously published books have been reissued, and several of her works, including *Mule Bone* (coauthored with Langston Hughes) have been published for the first time. *Their Eyes Were Watching God* has become part of the curriculum in high schools and colleges across the country. As a result, *Their Eyes* has now sold well over five million copies—more than a thousand times the number sold in Zora's lifetime. In 2005 Oprah Winfrey made a movie of *Their Eyes* starring Halle Berry, and in 2008 PBS aired a documentary called *Zora Neale Hurston: Jump at the Sun.* Each year, her hometown of Eatonville hosts the Zora Neale Hurston Festival of the Arts and Humanities, and Fort Pierce holds a Zora Fest.

Zora probably would have been pleased but not surprised by all this attention. After all, from the days when she claimed to be the moon's favorite child to the end of her life, Zora Neale Hurston never stopped believing in herself.

»»» The "Queen of the Harlem Renaissance" lies buried in an old cemetery in Fort Pierce, Florida, where Zora Neale Hurston died in poverty.

Zora Neale Hurston of Jacksonville, Fla. Awarded Second Prize for Short Story "Spunk" Awarded Second Prize for play "Color Struck."

»»» Zora won two second prizes in the 1925 *Opportunity* writing contest, one for her short story "Spunk" and another for her play *Color Struck*.

TWO "LIES" (FOLKTALES) COLLECTED IN FLORIDA BY ZORA NEALE HURSTON

«« ♦ »»

SIS SNAIL TOOK SICK in the bed, you know, and she didn't get better so after while she hollered for her husband and she told him, "Honey, I reckon you better go get the doctor for me. I'm so sick and don't look like I'm on the mend."

Brer Snail told her, "All right, I'll go get the doctor for you. Give me time to go get my hat." So Sis Snail rolled in the bed. After seven years she heard a noise at the door and she said, "I know that's my husband with the doctor, and I am so glad! Lord knows I'm so sick. Honey, is that you with the doctor?"

Brer Snail hollered back and told her, "Don't try to rush me! I ain't gone yet." It had took him seven years to get to the door.

THEY RAISE BIG VEGETABLES down around the Everglades. Yes, sir, that's rich land around down there. For instance, my old man planted sweet potatoes one year and when it come time to dig them potatoes, one of them had got so big they had to make a sawmill job out of it. They built a sawmill and put whole crews to work cutting up that big old sweet potato.

And so that year everybody in Florida had houses made out of sweet potato slabs. And what you reckon everybody ate that year? Well, they lived off of potato pone, made out of the sawdust from that great big old tater my old man raised.

ZORA TIME LINE

«« ◆ »»

1891 Zora, the fifth of eight surviving children in the Hurston family, is born in Notasulga, Alabama, on January 15.

1892 The Hurstons settle in the all-black town of Eatonville, Florida.

1897 John Hurston, Zora's father, is elected mayor of Eatonville.

1900 Zora is a star pupil at Eatonville's Hungerford School by this time.

1904 Lucy Potts Hurston, Zora's mother, dies on September 19; Zora is then sent to attend school and live in Jacksonville, Florida.

1905 John Hurston remarries in February but Zora doesn't get along with her stepmother, Mattie Moge Hurston.

1905–12 Mystery period of Zora's life; about all we know is that she sometimes worked as a maid in various Florida towns.

1912–15 Zora lives with various relatives including her brother Bob in Memphis, Tennessee.

1915 Zora goes to work as personal assistant to "Miss M," a singer in a traveling operetta troupe.

1917   Zora leaves Miss M's employ; she settles in Baltimore, where she has an emergency appendectomy and then attends night school and Morgan Academy.

1918   Zora moves to Washington, D.C., where she attends Howard Academy; her father dies in a car-train accident.

1919   Howard Academy awards Zora her high school diploma in May; in the fall, she enrolls in Howard University in Washington, D.C.

1921   Zora appears in print for the first time when the *Stylus* of Howard University publishes her poem "O Night" and her story "John Redding Goes to Sea."

1924   *Opportunity* magazine publishes Zora's story "Drenched in Light" in December.

1925   Zora moves to New York City during the heyday of the Harlem Renaissance; she wins awards in *Opportunity* magazine's writing contest.

1925–27   Zora attends Barnard College and also takes anthropology classes at Columbia University, both in New York City.

1926   Zora helps produce the one and only issue of *Fire!!* magazine in November.

1927   Zora travels to Florida to collect folklore; on May 19 she marries Herbert Sheen in Florida; in December, Zora begins receiving financial support from "Godmother" Charlotte Mason.

1928–30   Zora collects folklore in the southern United States and in the Bahamas; while on the road she is awarded her college diploma from Barnard, in 1928; she returns to New York having written a rough draft of the folklore manuscript that will become *Mules and Men*.

1931   In February, Zora fights with Langston Hughes over their play *Mule Bone*, ending their friendship; in July, Zora and Herbert Sheen's divorce is finalized.

1932   Zora stages her folk musical *The Great Day* at New York's John Golden Theatre, but it is a box-office failure; Godmother ends her financial support of Zora.

1933   Zora's "The Gilded Six-Bits" is published in the August issue of *Story* magazine; it leads to contracts from Lippincott for five books.

1934   In May, Zora's first novel, *Jonah's Gourd Vine*, is published.

1935   In October, Zora's folklore book *Mules and Men* is published.

1936   While in Haiti, Zora writes *Their Eyes Were Watching God* in seven weeks; she also begins *Tell My Horse*, her book about zombies, voodoo, and the folklore of Haiti and Jamaica.

1937   Zora's masterpiece, *Their Eyes Were Watching God*, is published in September.

1938   *Tell My Horse*, Zora's fifth book, is published in October and isn't well received.

1939   In June, Zora marries Albert Price III in Florida; in November her sixth book, *Moses, Man of the Mountain*, is published.

1941   Zora goes to work for the Hollywood movie studio Paramount, but she can't persuade the company to film any of her books.

1942   In November, Zora's autobiography, *Dust Tracks on a Road*, is published; it is her final book with Lippincott.

1943   Zora buys the houseboat *Wanago* and makes it her home; in November her divorce from Albert Price III is finalized.

1944   On January 18, Zora marries again; she and her third husband, James Howell Pitts, are divorced on October 31.

1945   Zora writes *Mrs. Doctor*, but Lippincott rejects it.

1947   Zora goes to Honduras to search for a "lost city" but spends most of her time there writing her new novel, *Seraph on the Suwanee*.

1948   Her new publisher, Scribner, issues *Seraph on the Suwanee* in October; it proves to be Zora's last published book.

1950   Zora's novel *The Lives of Barney Turk* is rejected by Scribner.

1951   Scribner rejects Zora's novel *The Golden Bench of God*.

1952   The *Pittsburgh Courier* hires Zora to cover the Ruby McCollum murder trial.

1955 *Herod the Great*, which Zora has worked on intensely for several years, is rejected by Scribner.

1958 Zora, whose health is failing, briefly teaches high school English in Fort Pierce, Florida.

1959 In October, Zora suffers a stroke; she moves to the St. Lucie County Welfare Home in Fort Pierce.

1960 On January 28, Zora suffers another stroke and dies; by then she has been largely forgotten as an author.

1975 In March, Alice Walker publishes "In Search of Zora Neale Hurston" in *Ms.* magazine, helping to launch a Zora revival.

1977 Robert Hemenway's book *Zora Neale Hurston: A Literary Biography* also helps spark a tremendous amount of renewed interest in Zora's work.

SOURCE NOTES

«« ♦ »»

ABBREVIATIONS AND SHORT TITLES USED IN NOTES

ZNH — Zora Neale Hurston

Dust — ZNH's autobiography, *Dust Tracks on a Road*

Hemenway — *Zora Neale Hurston: A Literary Biography* by Robert E. Hemenway

Rainbows — *Wrapped in Rainbows: The Life of Zora Neale Hurston* by Valerie Boyd

Letters — *Zora Neale Hurston: A Life in Letters*, edited by Carla Kaplan

Speak — *Speak, So You Can Speak Again: The Life of Zora Neale Hurston* by
      Lucy Anne Hurston

INTRODUCTION. "I'LL SAY MY SAY AND SING MY SONG"

    page ix "I'll say my say and sing my song": *Mules and Men*, p. 5.
                she believed the moon followed her: *Dust*, pp. 26–27.
        x "the real love affair of my life": *Dust*, pp. 205–11.
                largest royalty check...$943.75: Hemenway, p. 5.
                "four pennies": ZNH letter written March 18, 1951, in *Letters*, pp. 649–50.

xi Information about the rediscovery of ZNH's work appears in *Speak*, p. 7.

1. "SERVANTS ARE SERVANTS"

Much of the information about ZNH working as a maid at age fifty-nine comes from *Rainbows*, pp. 403–5.

2 "Employed as a maid in a Rivo Alto Island home…": James Lyons, "Famous Negro Author Working as Maid Here Just 'to Live a Little,'" *Miami Herald*, March 27, 1950.

3 "One of the nation's most accomplished Negro Women…": James Lyons, "Successful Author Working as a Maid," *St. Louis Post-Dispatch*, April 24, 1950.

3–4 "All I wanted was a little spending change" and "My working…": ZNH's March 1950 letter to Burroughs Mitchell, in *Letters*, p. 627.

2. "THE MOON RAN AFTER ME"

Nearly all of the material for this chapter comes from *Dust*.

5 actually born on January 15, 1891…: *Letters*, p. 773. Another date often given for ZNH's birth is January 7, 1891.

7 "The ordeal of share-cropping…": *Dust*, p. 7.
"There were plenty of orange…": *Dust*, p. 12.

8 ZNH's childhood belief that the moon followed her and her race with Carrie Roberts to see who the moon liked best are described in *Dust*, pp. 26–27.
"I was making little stories…" *Dust*, p. 53.

9 Grandma Sarah Potts…thought that Zora…: *Dust*, pp. 53–54.
some miniature friends…: *Dust*, pp. 54–58.
"It grew upon me…": *Dust*, pp. 27–28.

10 Lucy often said…"travel dust"…: *Dust*, pp. 22–23.
"Don't you want…?" to "turn out to be a mealy-mouthed rag doll…": *Dust*, 33–34.

11 "Jump at the sun...": *Dust*, p. 13.

A highlight of her childhood...: *Dust*, pp. 34–39.

13 "Perhaps I shall never...": *Dust*, p. 38.

14 Joe Clarke's general store... "lying sessions"...: *Dust*, pp. 45–51.

"go hide under the house...": ZNH letter of December 3, 1938, reproduced in *Letters*, pp. 417–18.

3. "IN SORROW'S KITCHEN"

Most of the information in this chapter originated in *Dust*.

16–17 ZNH describes Lucy's death in *Dust*, pp. 63–69.

18 Zora's siblings ranged in age...: The birthdates of ZNH's brothers and sister are given in *Letters*, p. 37.

"Jacksonville made me know...": *Dust*, p. 70.

21 "So I came back to my father's house...": *Dust*, p. 84.

22–24 "I was shifted from house to house...": *Dust*, p. 87.

24 "No matter how I resolved...": *Dust*, pp. 88–89.

a memorable incident that occurred around 1911...: *Dust*, pp. 75–78.

4. "THE GOLDEN STAIRS"

Dust and *Speak* provided most of the information for this chapter.

28 "Nothing can describe my joy...": *Dust*, 99.

29 Shortly after graduating from Meharry in 1913...: *Rainbows*, 67. This book was helpful regarding many other dates as well.

"My feet mounted up the golden stairs...": *Dust*, 101–2.

29–32 ZNH's adventures with "Miss M" and the operetta troupe are described in *Dust*, pp. 102–19.

31 "I have no race prejudice of any kind": *Dust*, p. 231.

32 "I learned that skins...": *Dust*, p. 191.

"find the road...": *Dust*, p. 122.

33 According to Maryland state law…: *Rainbows*, p. 75.

"[Literature is] my world…": *Dust*, p. 123.

35 "Dear Dean…": *Letters*, p. 54.

36 "Zora, you are Howard material.…"; "You can come and live": *Dust*, pp. 129–30.

39 An event that she witnessed in the barbershop…: *Dust*, pp. 134–36.

40 "For the first time since my mother's death…": *Dust*, p. 204.

41 "I know a place…": *Speak*, p. 9.

42 "John Redding Goes to Sea": This story can be found in *Speak*, p. 13.

45 "Drenched in Light": This story can be found in *Speak*, p. 9.

46 "So…the first week of January…": *Dust*, p. 138.

5. "A TOE-HOLD ON THE WORLD"

Most of the material for this chapter comes from *Dust*, Hemenway, *Rainbows*, and *Letters*.

48 "fun to be a Negro": *Rainbows*, p. 93.

50 "when Zora was there…": Hemenway, p. 61.

52 "Zora Neale Hurston is a clever girl…": *Rainbows*, p. 99.

53 "My Dear Mrs. Meyer…": ZNH to Annie Nathan Meyer, May 12, 1925, in *Letters*, p. 55.

53–54 "Almost nobody else could stop…": *Rainbows*, p. 114.

55 "Today I have 11 cents…": *Letters*, pp. 67–68.

on one occasion she actually stole money…: *Rainbows*, p. 105.

55–56 "My idea of Hell…": ZNH to Katherine L'Engle, February 1946, in *Letters*, pp. 540–41.

56 "shorthand was short on legibility…": *Rainbows*, p. 107.

57 "I have had some small success…": *Rainbows*, p. 103.

"I shall try to lay my dreaming aside…" ZNH to Annie Nathan Meyer, January 1926, *Letters*, 76–77.

"I do not wish to become Hurstized…" ZNH to Annie Nathan Meyer, December 13, 1925, *Letters*, pp. 71–72.

61 "took a roll of toilet paper..."; "She never made that boy feel bad...": *Rainbows*, 134.

"*Fire* has gone to ashes...": ZNH to Alain Locke, October 11, 1927, in *Letters*, pp. 109–10.

6. 1927

Most of the information for this chapter comes from *Dust*, Hemenway, *Rainbows*, and *Letters*.

66 "I did not have the right approach...": *Dust*, pp. 143–44.

67 "I found that what you obtained...": *Rainbows*, p. 146.

"It was not my happiest day....": *Dust*, p. 204.

"Yes, I'm married now...": ZNH to Dorothy West and Helene Johnson, May 22, 1927, in *Letters*, pp. 101–2.

68 "Zora was full of her work...": *Rainbows*, p. 150.

70 she committed the cardinal sin...: The story of ZNH plagiarizing material about Cudjo Lewis comes from Hemenway, pp. 96–100.

71 "Getting some gorgeous material...": ZNH to Langston Hughes, March 17, 1927, in *Letters*, p. 93.

73 "I stood before Papa Franz...": *Dust*, p. 144.

74 "Dear Bambino...": ZNH to Langston Hughes, September 21, 1927, in *Letters*, pp. 106–7.

7. "MOST GORGEOUS POSSIBILITIES"

Most of this chapter is based on material from *Dust*, *Rainbows*, Hemenway, and *Letters*.

81 "I believe I have almost...": ZNH to Langston Hughes, March 8, 1928, in *Letters*, pp. 112–14.

"I saw sudden death...": *Dust*, pp. 155–56.

83 "On the third night, I had dreams...": *Dust*, pp. 156–57.

84 "I am now writing music...": *Letters*, p. 147.

84 "I just had to know more...": *Dust*, p. 157.

85 "only [her] return ticket and 24 cents....": ZNH to Langston Hughes, October 15, 1929, in *Letters*, pp. 148–49.

"Well, I tell you, Langston...": ZNH to Langston Hughes, December 10, 1929, in *Letters*, pp. 154–55.

8. "YOU, LANGSTON HUGHES, CUT ME TO THE QUICK"

Most of the information for this chapter comes from Hemenway, *Rainbows*, and *Letters*.

90 "Darling my God-Flower...": *Letters*, pp. 187–89.

92 "I love you, Godmother....": *Rainbows*, pp. 203.

95 "I was just plain hurt....": *Letters*, pp. 201–4.

97 "[Zora] pushed her hat back..."; "I had to get up out of bed...": *Rainbows*, p. 215.

"DARLING GODMOTHER...": ZNH to Charlotte Mason, February 3, 1931, in *Letters*, p. 209.

98 "Godmother, for love...": *Letters*, pp. 221–23.

9. "IT COST $1.83 TO MAIL, AND I DID NOT HAVE IT"

This chapter is based mainly on material from *Dust*, *Rainbows*, Hemenway, and *Letters*.

101 "I firmly believe...": ZNH to Charlotte Mason, September 25, 1931, in *Letters*, pp. 226–30.

"My work is coming on most satisfactorily...": ZNH to Charlotte Mason, May 17, 1932, in *Letters*, pp. 255–56.

102 "Early in Feb. we sing...": ZNH to Charlotte Mason, January 6, 1933, in *Letters*, pp. 275–77.

105 "It cost $1.83 to mail...": *Dust*, p. 174.

108 "When I opened it and read...": *Dust*, p. 175.

110 "scared to <u>death</u> of reviews": ZNH to Carl Van Vechten, April 26, 1934, in *Letters*, p. 301.

10. "I WROTE IT IN SEVEN WEEKS": *THEIR EYES WERE WATCHING GOD*

Information for this chapter comes mainly from *Dust*, *Rainbows*, Hemenway, and *Letters*.

112 "One day eight people were trying to direct…": *Letters*, p. 317.

113 "the real love affair of my life": *Dust*, p. 207.

114 "He was tall, dark brown…": *Dust*, p. 205.

116 "I love myself when…" ZNH to Carl Van Vechten, December 10, 1934, in *Letters*, p. 324.

"That one thing I could not do…" *Dust*, p. 208.

117 "better even than Leadbelly": Hemenway, p. 212.

118 "gorgeous clothes"; "beautiful things": *Rainbows*, p. 278.

119–21 "I wrote *Their Eyes*…": *Dust*, p. 175.

121 "They saw other people…": *Their Eyes Were Watching God*, p. 153.

"I tried…[to embody] all the tenderness…": *Dust*, p. 211.

11. "I SHALL KEEP TRYING"

The sources for most of the material in this chapter are *Rainbows*, Hemenway, and *Letters*.

123 "an example of rank dishonesty"; "a fraud"; "[He] knows nothing…": Hemenway, pp. 241–42.

"Alain Leroy Locke is a malicious…": ZNH to James Weldon Johnson, February 1938, in *Letters*, pp. 413–14.

125 "Let's go!": *Rainbows*, p. 317.

"Aunt Zora doesn't have any business…": *Rainbows*, p. 325.

Zora and Albert were married…: Information about ZNH's marriage to Albert Price III appears in *Speak*, p. 25.

126 "They have strong winds on the Florida west coast.…": Bordelon, *Go Gator and Muddy the Water*, p. 76.

127 "I don't think it achieved…" ZNH, October 12, 1939, in *Letters*, pp. 422–23.

130 "I did not want to do it now…": ZNH, December 30, 1941, in *Letters*, pp. 463–65.

132 "the most unfortunate thing Zora ever wrote": Hemenway, p. xvii.

135 "I feel lucky to be under Max Perkins": *Letters*, p. 550.

12. "I HAD EXACTLY FOUR PENNIES"

Information for this chapter comes mainly from *Rainbows*, Hemenway, and *Letters*.

138 "Please help me…" ZNH to Fannie Hurst, February 10, 1949, in *Letters*, pp. 579–80.

141 "I had exactly four pennies": *Letters*, pp. 649–50.

142 "old cuss"; "He could not accept the reality…"; "We fought like tigers…": ZNH to Burroughs Mitchell, July 21, 1950, in *Letters*, pp. 630–32.

143 "The story I am burning to write…": ZNH to Carl Van Vechten, September 12, 1945, in *Letters*, pp. 528–30.

144 "under the spell of a great…": ZNH to Burroughs Mitchell, October 2, 1953, in *Letters*, pp. 702–4.

"Naturally, I am sorry…": ZNH to Burroughs Mitchell, August 12, 1955, in *Letters*, pp. 741–42.

147 "too well educated…": ZNH, June 27, 1957, in *Letters*, pp. 756–60.

"Discipline at Lincoln Park Academy…": ZNH, March 7, 1958, in *Letters*, pp. 765–68.

13. "NOTHING IS DESTRUCTIBLE":

THE REBIRTH OF ZORA NEALE HURSTON

Material for this chapter comes partly from *Rainbows* and *Speak*.

151 "Nothing is destructible…" *Dust*, p. 226.

155 *Their Eyes* has now sold well over five million copies…: *Speak*, p. 7.

Source Notes

«« ◆ »»

TWO "LIES" (FOLKTALES) COLLECTED
IN FLORIDA BY ZORA NEALE HURSTON

157–58 The Sis Snail "lie" appears in *Go Gator and Muddy the Water*, p. 78, and the sweet potatoes folktale is on page 77 of that book.

BIBLIOGRAPHY

«« ◆ »»

Bordelon, Pamela, ed. *Go Gator and Muddy the Water: Writings by Zora Neale Hurston from the Federal Writers' Project.* New York: Norton, 1999.

Boyd, Valerie. *Wrapped in Rainbows: The Life of Zora Neale Hurston.* New York: Scribner, 2003.

Hemenway, Robert E. *Zora Neale Hurston: A Literary Biography.* Urbana: University of Illinois Press, 1977.

Hurston, Lucy Anne. *Speak, So You Can Speak Again: The Life of Zora Neale Hurston.* New York: Doubleday, 2004.

Hurston, Zora Neale. *Dust Tracks on a Road.* New York: HarperCollins, 1996.

———. *Folklore, Memoirs, and Other Writings.* New York: Library of America, 1995.

———. *Mules and Men.* Bloomington: Indiana University Press, 1978.

———. *Their Eyes Were Watching God.* New York: Harper & Row, 1990.

Kaplan, Carla, ed. *Zora Neale Hurston: A Life in Letters.* New York: Doubleday, 2002.

Lyons, Mary E. *Sorrow's Kitchen: The Life and Folklore of Zora Neale Hurston.* New York: Charles Scribner's Sons, 1990.

Nichols, Charles H., ed. *Arna Bontemps–Langston Hughes Letters, 1925–1967.* New York: Dodd, Mead, 1980.

Walker, Alice, ed. *I Love Myself When I Am Laughing . . . and Then Again When I Am Looking Mean and Impressive: A Zora Neale Hurston Reader.* New York: Feminist Press, 1979.

IMAGE CREDITS

«« ◆ »»

INDEX

«« ♦ »»

Page numbers in *italics* refer to photos and their captions.

Index

«« ♦ »»

Index

«« ♦ »»

Index
«« ♦ »»

Index

«« ◆ »»